AN INTRODUCTION

TO THE

THEORY OF VALUE

MACMILLAN AND CO., Limited
LONDON · BOMBAY · CALCUTTA · MADRAS
MELBOURNE

THE MACMILLAN COMPANY
NEW YORK · BOSTON · CHICAGO
DALLAS · ATLANTA · SAN FRANCISCO

THE MACMILLAN COMPANY
OF CANADA, LIMITED
TORONTO

AN INTRODUCTION TO THE THEORY OF VALUE

ON THE LINES OF
MENGER, WIESER, AND BÖHM-BAWERK

BY

WILLIAM SMART, M.A., D.Phil., LL.D.

ADAM SMITH PROFESSOR OF POLITICAL ECONOMY, UNIVERSITY OF GLASGOW

MACMILLAN AND CO., LIMITED
ST. MARTIN'S STREET, LONDON
1931

Large Print Edition published 2013 by Skyler J. Collins.
Visit: www.skylerjcollins.com

Originally published in 1891.

ISBN-13: 978-1493555048
ISBN-10: 1493555049

To

W. S. H.

PREFACE TO THE SECOND EDITION, 1910

THIS little book was written in 1891, when I was fresh from my translations of Böhm-Bawerk and somewhat overborne, perhaps, by the ideas of his school. It has been out of print for many years, and, although often pressed to republish it, I refrained, for the reason that a busy life had prevented me returning to the later developments of that school. But I still feel, as I did when I wrote it, that my English-speaking colleagues have never given sufficient attention to that side of the one Theory of Value (for there is only one, however much individuals may emphasise the demand side or the supply side) which Jevons first laid stress on. Having now mortgaged my life to what seems to me the greater claim of writing the Economic Annals of the Nineteenth Century, the most I can do is to reprint the edition of 1891, with a few verbal alterations, submitting it as no more than it originally professed to be—an Introduction to the theory which lies at the centre of

Political Economy, and must occupy the mind of the young economist for many years of his apprenticeship. The few who may be interested to know what place I give, after many years of teaching, to doctrines which had so great a part in forming my economic views, will find it suggested, perhaps, in Appendix II., entitled "Theory of Value: the Demand Side." It is a summary of lectures, which I put into the hands of my students to be studied along with Book III. of the classic which has moulded modern economic thought, Professor Marshall's *Principles*.

WILLIAM SMART.

UNIVERSITY OF GLASGOW,
November, 1910.

PREFACE TO THE FIRST EDITION

THIS book has few pretensions to originality. The theory is that enunciated by Menger and Jevons, and worked out by Wieser and Böhm-Bawerk. I have done little more than take it out of its German setting, and pass it through my own mind. As the translator of Böhm-Bawerk's *Capital and Interest* and *The Positive Theory of Capital*, I may claim to have more than a superficial acquaintance with the work of the Austrian school, and this must form my credentials for the present *Introduction*. At the same time I must emphasise that it claims to be no more than an introduction. I do not consider that the last word on Value has been said by the Austrian school, but that seems to me no reason why the principles of the new theory should remain any longer beyond the reach of the ordinary English student. And in case it be said that I have stopped short of the most interesting part of the *Natürlicher Werth*, the application of the Value theory to the theory of

Distribution, I may explain that, in justice to Professor Wieser, I have preferred to put the translation of that most brilliant and suggestive book into the capable hands of one of my students.

WILLIAM SMART.

QUEEN MARGARET COLLEGE,
    GLASGOW

CONTENTS

CHAP.		PAGE
I.	Introductory	1
II.	The Analysis of Value	9
III.	The Difference Between Utility and Value	13
IV.	The Scale of Value	18
V.	The Marginal Utility	29
VI.	Difficulties and Explanations	35
VII.	Complementary Goods	42
VIII.	Subjective Exchange Value	47
IX.	From Subjective to Objective Value	52
X.	Price	55
XI.	Subjective Valuations the Basis of Price	61
XII.	Cost of Production	67
XIII.	From Marginal Products to Cost of Production	74
XIV.	From Cost of Production to Product	78
XV.	Conclusion	84
	Appendix I	87
	Appendix II	91
	Index	103

WRITERS AND BOOKS REFERRED TO

CARL MENGER (Professor in the University of Vienna), *Grundsätze der Volkswirthschaftslehre*, Vienna, 1871.

FRIEDRICH VON WIESER (Professor in the University of Prague), *Ueber den Ursprung und die Hauptgesetze des wirthschaftlichen Werthes*, Vienna, 1884.

Der natürliche Werth, Vienna, 1889, translated as *Natural Value*, Macmillan & Co., 1893.

EUGEN V. BÖHM-BAWERK (Honorary Professor in the University of Vienna), *Grundzüge der Theorie des wirthschaftlichen Güterwerths*, published in Conrad's *Jahrbücher*, 1886.

Geschichte und Kritik der Kapitalzius-theoriem, Innsbruck, 1884, translated as *Capital and Interest*, Macmillan & Co., 1890.

Positive Theorie des Kapitales, Innsbruck, 1889, translated as *The Positive Theory of Capital*, Macmillan & Co., 1891.

W. STANLEY JEVONS (Professor in University College, London), *The Theory of Political Economy*, 2d edition, Macmillan & Co., 1879.

CHAPTER I

INTRODUCTORY

THERE is an understanding among economists, dating at least as far back as Adam Smith, that, in economic science and discussion, the ordinary terms of the industrial world are to be used in the sense generally attached to them in that industrial world. In many respects this has been unfortunate: the science is bound for ever to a loose nomenclature. It is particularly unfortunate for English political economy, which has not the possibility, so enviable in German science, of combining a new predicate with an old stem in such a way that the combined word is exact and yet not unfamiliar. Hence very many terms in economics have a long and chequered history attached to them, according as economists, in writing their systems, have tried either to follow the usage of the market and the street, or to free themselves from the vexatious restraint.

No term affords a better illustration of this than the word Value. It is deeply rooted in popular conception and in popular speech. Of all words used in economic theory, it has most need of exact definition, because there the theory of value occupies the chief place. Yet the history of economic science is strewn with the wrecks of theories of value.

Every one knows Thornton's story of how Sydney Smith retired from the Political Economy Club, because his chief motive for joining it had been to discover what Value was, while all he had discovered was that the rest of the Club knew as little about the matter as he did! Every one, too, has smiled at Mill's statement, made in 1848, that there was nothing in the laws of value which remained for him or for any future writer to clear up. And many felt sympathy with Jevons when he threw the term overboard altogether, declaring that neither writers nor readers could avoid the confusion so long as they used the word.

But although it might be possible, by a very strict attention to proof sheets, to keep the word out of a book, it would not be possible to keep it out of the economist's mouth, any more than it would be to banish it from ordinary speech. And—happily, as it seems to me—the recent writings of the Austrian school have shown that we may retain the old familiar word, and yet attain the exactitude of scientific nomenclature.

There is a time-honoured classification to which is due much of the present confusion. In the *Wealth of Nations* (Book i. chap. iv.), occurs the following passage :

" The word Value, it is to be observed, has two different meanings, and sometimes expresses the utility of some particular object, and sometimes the power of purchasing other goods which the possession of that object conveys. The one may be called ' Value in use,' the other ' Value in exchange.' The things which have the greatest value in use have frequently little or no value in exchange ; and, on the contrary, those which have the greatest value in exchange have frequently little or no value in use. Nothing is more useful than water: but it will purchase scarce anything; scarce anything can be had in exchange for it. A diamond, on the contrary, has scarce any value in use, but a very great quantity of goods may frequently be had in exchange for it." [1]

This passage, like much else in Adam Smith, does not bear all that has been read into it by subsequent economists. It does not say that Use Value and Exchange Value are two great branches of one universal conception of Value. Nor does it say that they are entirely different conceptions. It merely says that the word has two different meanings. What concerns us, however, is the use that economists have generally made of this passage. They have quoted it with approval; shown that the two kinds of value do not by any means coincide; and have then gone on to discuss the latter as "economic value," or "what we mean by value in political economy." The best thing we can do, meantime, is to try to forget this old classification, and begin anew.

It scarcely requires proving that Value, in whichever of its various senses the word is used, does not express any inherent property of things. Very often, indeed, we can scarcely help thinking of Value as a quality of a material object,—particularly when the object is one of universal desire, such as gold coin.

---

[1] The division is as old as Aristotle. "Of everything which we possess there are two uses both belonging to the thing as such, but not in the same manner; for one is the proper and the other the improper or secondary use of it. For example, the shoe is used for wear, and it is used for exchange; both are uses of the shoe."—*Politics* (Jowett), § 9.

But Walker's monetary formula, "Money is that money does," may remind us that the value even of gold coin is given it by the service it renders in a highly organised community, and that, if to any substitute can be given the confidence that gold commands, the same value will attach to it—"attach" but not "inhere." Sometimes, again, value is so strongly a personal experience that we are tempted to think of it as purely a subjective matter, and this is particularly the case among people who understand Ruskin's famous words, "There is no Wealth but Life." The different value set upon any work of art by different individuals, classes, or nations, is sufficient proof of this.

But although it is almost impossible to use the term without suggesting an inherent property,[1]

---

[1] "Value is the life-giving power of anything; cost, the quantity of labour required to produce it; price, the quantity of labour which its possessor will take in exchange for it. 'Value' signifies the strength, or 'availing' of anything towards the sustaining of life, and is always twofold; that is to say, primarily, intrinsic, and secondarily, effectual. Intrinsic value is the absolute power of anything to support life. A sheaf of wheat of given quality and weight has in it a measurable power of sustaining the substance of the body; a cubic foot of pure air, a fixed power of sustaining its warmth; and a cluster of flowers of given beauty, a fixed power of enlivening or animating the senses and heart. It does not in the least affect the intrinsic value of the wheat, the air, or the flowers, that men refuse or despise them. Used or not, their own power is in them, and that particular power is in nothing else. But in order that this value of theirs may become effectual, a certain state is necessary in the recipient of it. The digesting, breathing, and perceiving functions must be perfect in the human creature before the food, air, or flowers can become of their full value to it. The production of effectual value, therefore, always involves two needs: first, the production of a thing essentially useful; then the production of the capacity to use it."—*Munera Pulveris*, i. § 12.

I quote this passage, partly on account of its suggestiveness, partly to show how impossible it would be to reconcile any such definition of value either with ordinary language or with economic science.

Value in all its forms implies a relation. The word seems to arise fundamentally in the relation of Means to End, and will accordingly take various forms according to the " end " conceived of. This end may be, directly, the Wellbeing of man, whether conceived of as the ideal good of humanity, or the social ideal current at the time, or the realisation of individual character, or merely the gratification of individual desire. Or it may be some mechanical or technical result, which has no direct reference to personal wellbeing, or at least admits of being considered, for the moment, as a merely objective or intermediate result. Corresponding to these two classes of " ends," we may divide the phenomena of value into Subjective—or Personal—Value and Objective Value. The expressions are not by any means perfect,[1] but they are the terms generally used by the Austrian school, and they are perhaps the best we can get.

Value, in the subjective sense, we may call, generally, the importance which a good is considered to possess with reference to the wellbeing of a person. In this sense, a good is valuable to me when I consider that my wellbeing is associated with or dependent on the possession of it—that it " avails " towards my wellbeing.

[1] For instance—to say nothing of the fact that all economic ends must be subjective—of the four ways indicated above in which Wellbeing may be conceived, the three first may be considered objective as compared with the subjective fourth, while the wellbeing of man generally—particularly the ideal good—may very well be called the only objective end in contrast to the accident of a technical result. But, as it is impossible to keep the economic vocabulary clear of the philosophical, we may be satisfied if these names are definite enough to keep before our minds the broad lines of the division indicated above.

Value, in the objective sense, is a relation of power or capacity between a good and an objective result. In this sense, a good has value when it has the power of producing—or "avails" towards—some objective effect. There are, consequently, as many objective values as there are objective effects. Thus while the subjective value of coal to me is the amount of "good" I get from the fire, its objective value is the temperature which it maintains in the room, or the amount of steam it can raise in the boiler, or the money it brings me if I sell it. This kind of value is very much synonymous with the word "power" or "capacity"; it is as common to speak of "heating power" as of "heating value."

There is no doubt that "Value" is generally used, in ordinary language and thought, in both these senses. But there is also no doubt that powers or values of the latter sort *in general* do not enter into economic study at all. We have nothing to do with the heating value of coal, or the resisting power of iron, or the fattening properties of oil-cake; these are purely physical or technical matters. But, inside this class of Objective Values, there is one species which has a peculiarly economic interest, and that is, the "power of exchange" or "purchasing power." By this is meant the capacity or power of a good to obtain other goods in exchange. Of course, the word "power" here is also misleading. No good has this power in itself. It is, at best, a power conferred on goods by the complex machinery of an organised economic community, and it does not exist outside of a system of exchange. It is a power that lies in the connection or relation of two things, and not in either of the things. Jevons very well called it a

Ratio of Exchange. But it is purely an "objective" relation as we have defined it; as objective, for instance, as heating power. When the quarter of wheat in the market exchanges for 25s., we say, indifferently, that the "exchange value of the wheat is 25s.," or that "the purchasing power is 25s.," or that "the ratio of exchange between the wheat and the shillings is as 25 to 1."

It has been the ambition of economists to explain all kinds of value from a single universal conception, but so far the result has only been to group heterogeneous elements under a common name. It might be possible, perhaps, to connect them all under the general conception of "that which avails," or under the relation of Means to End; but whether much is gained by this for economic science is doubtful.[1]

Here, at any rate, we shall follow the line which has led to good results among the Austrian economists, and consider Subjective and Objective Value in general as two independent conceptions accidentally associated in common usage.

But, while this seems true, as regards Subjective and Objective value *in general*, we shall find that there is a close and necessary connection between subjective value and that one branch of objective value just referred to, namely, Objective *Exchange* Value. In what follows it will be shown that this latter Value, while, in itself, an objective, and, as it were, a mechanical power, is a superstructure on the

---

[1] Böhm-Bawerk, like Neumann, while acknowledging that the two conceptions have many internal and external relations, and that both spring undoubtedly from one common root, thinks that any more universal conception, which should embrace them both, would be *ganz leer und schattenhaft*.

subjective or personal estimates of value put upon goods by buyers and sellers within a market. In short, we shall have to vindicate, or at least defend, Jevons' assertion, now become a text of the Austrian School, that " Value depends entirely on Utility."

From what has been said the reader will be prepared for the claim of this school, in opposition to Adam Smith and many of his successors, that, when the word Value is used without qualification, it should mean Subjective—or Personal—Value, and not Purchasing Power. The first and the main work of the theory of value, then, is to inquire into the nature, causes, and standard of Subjective Value.

CHAPTER II

THE ANALYSIS OF VALUE

POLITICAL Economy is based on the analysis of economic conduct. As has been said, we are not at liberty to lay down new categories or even to give new names to economic phenomena. We have to take our categories and our vocabulary alike from the industrial and commercial world, and our most original work in this department is no more than the interpretation of a life which is, for the most part, unconscious of its own laws: a category of " the useful " or " the valuable " which practical people did not recognise as containing useful and valuable things and no other, would be quite unscientific. True, the economist has sometimes to show that the practical world is unfaithful to its own principles, but he can do so only after extended study of the economic organism has yielded these principles. The theory of value, therefore, must begin with a careful analysis of what the word means in the mouths of ordinary people.

A man values food, clothing, shelter, and the like, because they minister to his physical life, and he values music and books because they minister to what he calls his " higher life." As a nation, we value our service rifle because it can kill at so many hundred yards, and many forms of art and literature are highly valued because they minister to corrupt desires and moral decay. A collector values a piece of ugly china because it is old and rare, just as most women value their diamonds because everybody cannot wear diamonds.

Taking these instances as fairly typical, and collating the common ideas out of them, we seem to learn three things about value.

First, that, in probably the great majority of cases, the word has some direct or indirect reference to human life. On the whole, one would be inclined to say that the root idea of the valuable is that which *avails towards life*.

Second, that men, as not only imperfect in nature but erring in judgment, have made an easy extension of the term "human life" to cover "human desire," and count things valuable because they satisfy some want or other. The economic "want" is not necessarily a rational or a healthy want—and political economy, as primarily analytic, must not be censured for the statement, nor condemned as if it approved of the fact—but simply a want, and the things which satisfy such wants we call "goods." The *desirable* is interpreted in economics by the *desired*.

Third, that the element of scarcity somehow plays a large part in many, and seems to have a share in all, estimates of value.

Were it not for this element of scarcity one might conclude that the "valuable" and the "useful" were synonymous terms. Few writers have been careful to keep the two conceptions sufficiently separate, and the distinction which we have now to draw, while contained in Ricardo, was not scientifically formulated till the appearance of Menger's *Grundsätze* in 1871.

The economically Useful is that which is capable of satisfying the want of man—always meaning by "want" no more than "desire."[1] Corresponding with this conception, economically, is that of the "Good."[2] To constitute a good, four things, according to Menger, are required: (1) a human want, (2) certain properties in an object which make it capable of satisfying a human want, (3) the knowledge of this capability, (4) power to dispose of this object in the satisfaction of want.

In these two conceptions, the Useful and the Good, there is no reference to scarcity.

We shall find the Valuable separating itself naturally from the Useful if we look at what are called the free gifts of nature. Air, water, light, are recognised by every one as useful. But are they valuable? Most people—economists without knowing it—would answer in the negative, although certainly there is reason to suspect that they base this answer on the fact that they "could not get anything for them." Again, those scarce things which we seem to value just because they are scarce

---

[1] "Anything which an individual is found to desire and to labour for must be assumed to possess for him utility. In the science of Economics we treat men, not as they ought to be, but as they are."—Jevons, *Theory*, 2d Edition, p. 41.

[2] It is one of the difficulties of our economic vocabulary that, where we wish to express the singular of "goods," we have to use "commodity" or some such word. In my translations, I have made no scruple of rendering the honest German *Gut* by its literal equivalent, and it is in this sense that the word is used above and throughout this book. It will be noted in what follows that there is a difference between simple goods and "economic goods."

(as rare statues, pictures, books, coins, wines made from grapes of one limited locality, etc., to use Ricardo's examples), have always a background of usefulness, as satisfying some social, or class, or individual desire.

Evidently Usefulness or Utility is the larger conception of the two, and embraces Value. But if all valuable things are useful, while all useful things are not valuable, value must emerge at some particular limiting point of utility. Value, then, will be based on utility—utility limited in some particular way, but still utility.[1]

---

[1] It is perhaps a pity on two grounds that the word "utility" should have been adopted by economic science :—(1) that the word seems to suggest things really useful, when it means no more than things desired, bought, and sold ; (2) that it has so often suggested to shallow thinkers that Political Economy is a "sordid science" whose investigations do not go beyond mere material considerations

CHAPTER III

THE DIFFERENCE BETWEEN UTILITY AND VALUE

UTILITY and not Value, says Wieser, is "the supreme principle of all economy; where value and utility come into conflict, utility must conquer." The statement is suggestive. The economic goal of civilisation is to turn the whole natural environment of man from a relation of hostility or indifference into a relation of utility. Certain goods we have from nature without money and without price, and the incessant effort of the industrial world is *in the direction* of bringing all goods nearer to that category. Indeed, some of the necessaries of life have already been brought so nearly to that condition that states and municipalities occasionally pay the small remaining price, and distribute them as heaven does the rain. The effort to improve production generally is nothing else than the effort to multiply utilities and, as consequence, to reduce their price. For, while value reflects utility, the mirror is too small to hold all the picture. To use Wieser's words again, "Value is the calculation-form of utility"—an expression which will be appreciated if we realise how impossible it is to estimate the utility of a harvest, how easy to calculate its amount and its price.

Value, then, is a much less comprehensive conception, and does not emerge till a certain limitation is put upon this utility. But the limitation in question is not an arbitrary one. To drain a river of a few hundred gallons, or even to drain it all but a few hundred gallons, will not necessarily give the remainder any value. To change utility into value there must be, not only a capability of satisfying want, but a felt dependence of some want on the particular good containing the utility. The relation of value to utility, in fact, may be described as the relation of a positive condition to a capability. As capable of quenching thirst, all water is useful, but it does not obtain any value till some limitation of the available quantity makes it the indispensable *condition* of a satisfaction. The water led into a city may come from a stream which, as a whole, flows to the sea unvalued, but, in the city, it conditions the wellbeing of thousands of people, and obtains a value from the satisfaction of wants that are conditioned by it.

If, then, the distinction between Value and Utility, which seems essential to clearness of thinking, is to be maintained, it will be by attaching the former to an indispensable and felt condition, the latter to a general capability of ministering to human wellbeing.

Thus we may say that, while utility is the importance which a good possesses as generally *capable* of ministering to the wellbeing of a subject, Value is the importance which a good possesses as the *indispensable condition* of the wellbeing of a subject. Or more fully: Value is the importance which a good acquires as the recognised condition of something that makes for the wellbeing of a subject, and would not be obtainable without the good.[1] It cannot be too firmly grasped then, that the relation between utility and value is *quantitative*, and that the same thing may or may not have value according to change of circumstances, or difference in points of view and comparison.

To put this in another way. The first thing the economist sees in man is, that he stands in a relation of want to the world outside him. Economically, man is a complex of wants, some physical, some intellectual, some æsthetic, and so on. And, the higher man rises in the scale of spiritual being, the more numerous and varied are his wants. But want is in itself, if not a painful feeling, at least, a feeling of incompleteness. As an animal, man knows instinctively, and, as an intellectual being, he learns by experience, that certain things or arrangements in the outside world are the objects which such a feeling craves: as they are supplied to the organism in which the wants inhere, the feelings of want, gradually or immediately, fade away, and feelings of satisfaction or pleasure supervene. In time the satisfaction fades, the wants reappear, and the process begins over again. Thus the wants of man's life, whether these wants are wise or unwise, natural or acquired, constitute a demand for satisfaction. Each individual has his quota of wants, and the sum total of all wants makes the community's demand for satisfaction. To meet this demand the working portion of the community is set producing. The whole end and

---

[1] Menger's definition is " Die Bedeutung, welche concrete Güter oder Güterquantitäten für uns dadurch erlangen, das wir in der Befriedigung unserer Bedürfnisse von der Verfügung über dieselben abhängig zu sein uns bewusst sind."—*Grundzüge*, p. 78.

aim of the industrial organisation of society is to put the matter and forces of nature into shapes capable of satisfying this demand, and these shapes, now recognised as "good," society significantly calls "Goods."

If, in any class of goods, the supply is not sufficient to meet this demand for satisfaction (whether the demand be that of the individual or of the community), some want goes unsatisfied; the painful feeling of emptiness points to some good or other as the condition of a certain wellbeing; the relation of dependence between person and thing is established, and value emerges. If, on the other hand, the supply of any class of goods is so great that every demand is met, and yet there is such a surplus that no ordinary waste will cause scarcity, then no want goes unsatisfied, and value does not emerge. Suppose that a housewife is in the habit of using ten gallons of water a day for various domestic purposes. If the well, from which she draws her supply, holds just ten gallons and no more, then every gallon is the condition of a definite use or satisfaction, and every gallon has a value—the test being that, if one gallon is lost, some domestic purpose is not served. But if the well yields twenty gallons, the loss of even ten gallons involves no loss of wellbeing to the housewife; no want goes unsatisfied; no value emerges. And, again, if the wants increase to eleven, or the supply sinks to nine gallons, certain wants go unsatisfied, and value emerges.

One begins to see that the centre of value is within us. It is only by association that we transfer to goods the "value" which we get through the consumption of them. We attach importance to goods only as we find that our life is incomplete or impossible without them. Thus water, air, etc., being, in their totality, conditions of our life, we attach value to them *as a whole*, and, indeed, speak of them as " infinitely valuable." But we do not attach value to any individual portion of them, because, where there is enough to allow of waste, our lives are not *dependent* on any individual portion.

Thus it is that the theory of value lies at the basis of all economic theory. The only goods we " economise "—the goods which alone are objects of economic attention—are the goods which are insufficient, or just sufficient, to meet our wants. Contrasted with these are the " free gifts of nature," meaning by the expression such things, adapted to man's use, as are given us by nature in superfluous abundance. As goods which we economise, therefore, are the only goods which we recognise as *conditioning* our satisfaction, we may say that, while all goods, by definition, have utility, only economic goods have value.[1]

---

[1] In view of the loose way in which we use " economic " and " economise," Menger's definitions are worth remembering. When men recognise that their wellbeing is bound up with the command over certain goods within certain periods of time, and that such goods are likely to be insufficient for their demand, their impulse is (1) to get such goods into their possession or disposal ; (2) to preserve the useful properties of the same ; (3) to decide which are their more important and which their less important wants, and to satisfy the former only ; and (4) to so dispose of the goods as to get the greatest possible result or satisfaction on the whole, and to obtain every individual result with the smallest possible expenditure. " The activity men direct to those ends, in its totality, we call their ' economy,' and the goods which stand in these quantitative relations, as the exclusive objects of that economy, we call ' economic goods.' "—*Grundsätze*, chap. ii. § 3.

CHAPTER IV

THE SCALE OF VALUE

IF the cause of any good having value is that the satisfaction of some want is dependent upon it, the degree or amount of value must, one would imagine, be measured by the importance of the dependent want; that is to say, by the amount of wellbeing its satisfaction conditions. But here most people will hesitate. They would, probably, be willing to admit that utility is, in a general way, the cause of value, or, like Ricardo, that utility is " absolutely essential to exchangeable value." But they are shaken in this belief when they remember that things which seem to be of great utility, like salt, are little valued, while things of little utility, like diamonds, are very highly valued, and are told that it is this contradiction which led to the distinction between " value-in-use " and " value-in-exchange "—practically to the abandonment of the former.

We have here a heritage from our earlier economic science. Old classifications are more easily dismissed than got rid of; and it may not be wasted time to point out in this chapter how Adam Smith hopelessly confused utility and value by the introduction of the hermaphrodite " use-value."

We have already defined the economically Useful as that which is capable of satisfying the want of man. If utility, then, is relative to human want, it would seem that, before pronouncing on what has great and what has little utility, we must classify the various wants, and arrange them on some sort of scale. The familiar expression, however, "One man's meat is another man's poison," might be taken as a text to show the difficulty of classifying wants. There are certain wants which require periodical or continuous satisfaction, such as the needs of food and warmth. These wants seem to tie us to the earth, and they keep us perpetually in mind of our physical limitations. However high we soar into the regions of spirit, hunger and cold bring us to earth again; and, if these wants are not satisfied, the animal nature asserts itself, and we are ready to sell our birthright for a mess of pottage. Such wants, then, are fundamental and universal—instinctively we call them "needs." But there are two very notable circumstances connected with them. One is that they are limited. More meat than the body requires clogs the wheels of life; more than a certain amount of clothes is a burden. The other is that these fundamental and limited wants are precisely the ones for which nature makes the most abundant provision. There must be many millions of people who have never known what hunger is except by hearsay, nor imagined the torturing cold of a night on the street.

But, on this simple and, to a certain extent, measurable basis of necessary, universal, and limited wants, we rear a superstructure of other kinds of want. Of the distinctively human wants, there are many that become "necessary" from the individual or social development of intellectual and spiritual beings. Beyond these, again, there are innumerable desires, caprices, and follies. These, however, are not in the least limited in their demands: here "the appetite grows by what it feeds on." As civilisation and as wealth progress, not only does the old circle of want expand, but new wants awaken. This makes classification of such wants all but impossible. Between the wants of the savage or the child and those of the educated man or delicately nurtured woman, there is a long gradation of almost infinite fineness. How are we to put in one category the hunger and thirst which are satisfied, among members of one class, by bacon and beer, and, among members of another class, by stately dinners and rare vintages; or the "love of dress," which in one sphere demands "a black silk and a gold brooch," in another, diamonds and old lace? Yet the fact that goods may be purchased at prices from a farthing upwards, proves that the community *has* classified its wants in some sort of way. We find exchange existing in all communities, even the simplest, and exchange presupposes that we have already arranged our wants on a scale, and said that the satisfaction of such and such wants confers a high value on the goods which satisfy them, and the satisfaction of such and such a low value. What is the principle of this scale?

Adam Smith, and all who have followed him in paraphrasing his text "a diamond has scarce any value in use," certainly referred to a scale of wants, and considered this scale so important, and so universally recognised, that they had to separate off the value measured by it (use value) from the value measured by money or barter (exchange value). But they did so instinctively, and, if we inquire what this scale is, we have some difficulty in translating the instinctive expression.

There is a rough, but sometimes convenient, division of goods into Necessaries, Comforts, and Luxuries. Corresponding with this classification of goods, we might consider the physical needs satisfied by "necessaries" as the most important; and in the first rank of utilities, therefore, we should put goods necessary to sustain life, such as food, clothes, shelter. Next would come health and fulness of life, and in the second rank of utilities we should put good food, good clothes, good shelter. Last we should put the refinements or the artificial appetites of life, and, corresponding with these, we should have music and pictures, liquor, tobacco, and so on. It is easy to see that the sanction or principle of this scale is a negative one. It is not based on the satisfaction we get from goods, but on the consequences which will ensue to our lives if these wants go unsatisfied. Food is in the first rank of goods, because here death follows unsatisfied need. Tobacco is in a subordinate place, because the want of it causes, at worst, discomfort. And diamonds come in the lowest rank of useful goods because the loss of them involves a quite trifling loss of wellbeing. Here is a scale of wants with a definite enough principle.

But it is a scale adapted to circumstances so simple as to have no resemblance to any known form of society. Possibly the economists' favourite classic, Robinson Crusoe, has had something to do with the making of it. Certainly there never was a people who divided out their labour to satisfy successively the wants of such a scale, not producing anything for fulness of life till all had the necessaries, nor anything for pleasure till all had the necessaries of efficiency. Such a division of labour would evidence a higher level of reason and self-restraint than our communities have reached, since it would be founded on a deliberate theory of social life. The very suggestion that the loss of diamonds is "trifling" would justify the reproach one has sometimes to bear, that "it is well seen political economy was written by men!" The fact remains that this is nobody's scale: the poorest savage, the worst paid mill-girl, the most refined woman, will put ornament only second to bare necessaries.

Yet it seems that it must have been a scale something like this by which the older economists measured utility. In the interpretation they gave to "use value," they assumed that utility is relative to mere physical life. Those who speak of diamonds having no use-value, and of food as having infinite use-value, must be drawing their ideas, not from the life of men but from the life of cattle. It is possible to draw out a scientific catalogue of what things and amounts and conditions will put a sheep or bullock into the best condition for the market, just as it is possible to consider the human labourer as a force of so many foot-pounds. But the economic end of the sheep is—mutton, while the economic end of labour is—the labourer. That is to say, the "life" by which economists, as distinguished from butchers, must measure utility, is the life of a spiritual being for whom and towards whom all economic effort exists. To such a being, it is inconceivable that bread should have the highest use-value and diamonds none at all.

Compared with this purely theoretical scale, let us inquire of facts as to the scale which men in ordinary life adopt as regards goods.

Consciously or unconsciously, every man whose means or wealth or resources are more limited than his wants—and this is, practically, the case with human beings generally—has a scale of wants in his mind when he arranges his expenditure. On the basis of this scale, he satisfies what are his more urgent wants, and leaves the less urgent unsatisfied. But which are the more urgent wants on his scale? Are they determined by anything like the classification just mentioned? If so, how is it that a tramp with sixpence in his pocket will spend threepence on a bed in a lodging house, a penny on bread, and twopence on tobacco?

This by itself is sufficient to show that Adam Smith's graduation of wants is quite misleading in the present connection. When we ask about the "degree" or "urgency" of any individual want, we get no information by determining to what class or kind it belongs—whether, for instance, it is the need for a necessary or the desire for a luxury. The craving for food, as has been suggested, belongs so conspicuously to the first class of wants, that we do not so often speak of "wants" of subsistence, as of "needs" of subsistence. The desire for liquor, again, some people would scarcely dignify by the name of "want" at all. Yet many people will attach as much importance to the one as to the other. If we are to judge by his expenditure, the working man may graduate his wants thus: bread, house room, liquor, tea, tobacco, clothes, meat; while a rich man may spend more on his horses than he does on his house, and his grocer's bill may be less than his florist's. The fact seems to be that, with the scale of wants which each man makes for himself, the graduation by classes or kinds has very little to do. From the consideration already pointed out, that certain wants are fundamental, necessary, and universal, the class must, indeed, have something to do with it, but the other two considerations, the limited nature of these wants and the abundance of provision for them in most communities, throw the consideration of necessity quite into the background.

There is one case, however, where Adam Smith's scale comes nearly true;—where the income is just sufficient, and no more, to cover the barest wants of man as a living being. If a seamstress has to sustain life on a shilling a day, she will take care to dispose of the shilling in such a way that she spends on food just enough to keep life in, on clothes, enough to keep her warm, while the meanest roof that will keep out the rain will satisfy her "want of shelter." And, in proportion as we approximate to this direst poverty, will the class have more to do with the scale. Even the seamstress, however, will probably "jump" the class of comforts, and spend her last penny on the highest concrete want among the luxuries of the poor, tea.

This was the first mistake made by the older economists in the matter: it based "use-value" on a false or, at least, an unduly limited, conception of utility. The second—and more subtle—was in keeping no clear distinction between this utility and the so-called "use-value." For want of this distinction, it was overlooked that, in the relation between wants and goods in which value emerges, the *supply* of goods plays a part. Value emerges when a good becomes the condition of a satisfaction ; it is conferred by the dependence of a *felt* want, not of a *possible* one. Hunger, for instance, —understanding by that the overmastering craving which puts all other feelings into the background— is not a felt want if food lies around like the manna on the Israelites' plain. The nearer we get to making any object of want similar to a gift of nature, the less value has that object—not that its capability of use is any less, but that the abundance of supply has abolished the relation of *dependence*. A want never felt, would, of course, not be a want at all. But a trifling want unsupplied attains an importance for wellbeing which elevates it into a cause of value. Now, in the case of goods adapted to satisfy the necessary and universal wants of mankind, as no man can escape from these wants, there is always a large and steady market for these goods, and we call them " necessaries." Wherever we have such a market in economic life, we may be sure that the brains of men and the resources of nature have been taxed to the utmost to make the supply abundant and cheap. Hence the tendency of economic progress is to assure the satisfaction of these fundamental and limited wants ; in proportion as this is done, do men escape from that dependence which gives value : and thus many goods tend to come nearer to the free gifts of nature—their value falls and falls. The old theory, then, in taking hunger as the type of the most urgent want, was not dealing with wants, but with *possibilities* of want. Want is, at bottom, a feeling of incompleteness. It may indicate something wanting to our physical organism which, if entirely unsupplied, will cause death. But if a few mouthfuls be sufficient to make this want disappear for the moment, and if there be no probability of these mouthfuls ever being absent, we have been too hasty in giving it the highest rank among human wants. To consider food as having the highest use value because the want of food means death, is like estimating the greatness of a danger by the loss of life which it might cause, without considering the precautions taken to prevent it: it reminds one of the schoolboy's proposition, "Pins have saved many thousands of lives—By people not swallowing them."

To sum up. In assuming that bread and water had a higher "use-value" than iron, iron than gold, gold than diamonds, the earlier economists evidently referred to a theoretical scale of wants which is not recognised by any man as *his* scale; and, as they could not ignore the fact that practical men, in making their valuations, seemed to put diamonds above gold, gold above iron, and iron above bread, they had to divide off their so-called "use-value" sharply from the value which ruled the economical transactions of the world, and to call the latter "exchange value." The modern economist says that the phenomenon of bread possessing little value and diamonds much value, is not in contradiction with the theory that value depends entirely on utility. Bread is little thought of, and diamonds much thought of, because, when all the circumstances are taken into account—the circumstance of limitation of want and the circumstance of provision for want—the importance to concrete human want of the one is little, and of the other is much.

Note

The Austrian writers, whose economics are strongly coloured by the utilitarian psychology, usually put the matter in the following way. The course of the satisfaction of a want may be represented by a diminishing scale. Of most wants, material and intellectual alike, it is true that the pleasure got from the first draught of satisfaction is the keenest. The complete satisfaction, then, of any want might be represented by a graduated scale diminishing to zero—beyond zero, the satisfaction turning into satiety and disgust.

If we combine this scale with the other alluded to in the text—that which has the negative sanction of loss of well-being—we get a scheme like the following:

I	II	III	IV	V	VI	VII	VIII	IX	X
10									
9	9								
8	8	8							
7	7	7	7						
6	6	6	.	6					
5	5	5	.	5	5				
4	4	4	4	4	4	4			
3	3	3	.	3	3	.	3		
2	2	2	.	2	2	.	2	2	
1	1	1	1	1	1	.	1	1	1
0	0	0	0	0	0	0	0	0	0

Here the Roman figures indicate classes or kinds of wants, the Arabic, the concrete wants, or part wants, in each class. We thus see at a glance that, the more important the class, the more important are the concrete wants that stand highest in the class: that, even in the highest class, there are concrete wants which are outweighed by concrete wants of almost every other lower class: and that there are classes of want, like IV and VII, which are not satisfied gradually, as in the assuaging of hunger, but where want breaks off at a high level and does not emerge again till wants of much inferior classes have been met.

As an illustration, this scheme has a certain value, but it suggests more objections perhaps than it settles. The division of wants into kinds or classes, whether the principle of that division be determined by the nature of the sensations or by the objects which satisfy them, requires a better psychological basis than has yet been demonstrated. For instance, a generic want like that called Needs of Subsistence, is about as vague a conception as could well be imagined. And, again, on the " calculus of pleasure and pain," the satisfaction of want generally involves degrees and levels of physical, intellectual, and æsthetic feeling which cannot be represented by any such simple diagram. For these reasons—and also because the theory of value is not accredited by seeming to rest so much on a utilitarian psychology—I have not included the *Sättigungscala* in the text. There are some ingenious and interesting calculations on the subject in Wieser (*Natürlicher Werth*, p. 27), which I have added in the Appendix.

CHAPTER V

THE MARGINAL UTILITY

THUS far we have seen that, utility being the general relation in which all goods, by their very definition, stand to human wellbeing, value is that higher, more intimate, more limited relation in which some particular importance to human wellbeing is conditioned by the having or losing of some particular good, and a relation of actual dependence is established between the want and the good. We pass now to the positive consideration of the measurement of value.

If one good stands over against one want—that is to say, if the satisfaction of a single want is dependent on the possession of or power over a single good—there is no difficulty: the value is the entire utility which the good affords in the given case.

But the estimates of value which practically concern us are not so simple. We must face the fact that most goods which we have to value are not single articles, but many goods of the same kind—stocks of goods—and that, at the same time, most goods are capable of satisfying several wants. Water, for instance, may be used for drinking, for washing, for cooling, for ornamental fountains, etc., as books may be used for reading, for lending, for ornament, for packing, for waste paper, and so on. But these are uses of very different importance, and the question is: Which of these utilities is it that determines the value? This important point cannot be too plainly put, and it will be wise to follow the Austrian writers generally in taking the risk of being tedious rather than of being obscure.

A sailor and his dog, the sole survivors from a wreck, have been tossing on a raft for many days. Land is in sight, but still far away, and the food is reduced to a couple of biscuits. Both man and dog are equally famished, and it becomes evident that, unless each gets a biscuit, one of them will not live to reach the shore. Here we are confronted with the opposing claims of two wants, that of the sailor and that of his dog; and, as the sailor is, presumably, the valuer, the two wants are of very different importance to him. The question is, What measures the value of the biscuits? According to our formula, the answer will be found by ascertaining which is the dependent want—which is the satisfaction that the biscuits condition.

At first sight, one would say that the actual destination of the biscuits determined this; but that would be to say that two exactly similar biscuits, both available to the one man, and available under exactly similar conditions, were of different value. In this dilemma, one little consideration easily determines the point. If one of the biscuits were lost, which want would go unsatisfied? For the want which is satisfied if the good is present, and unsatisfied if it is not, is evidently the dependent want.[1]

---

[1] There are two typical cases where valuations are made:—where a man values something he *has*, with the view of parting with it (in selling, giving, lending, etc.), and where he values something he *has*

The dependent want, in this case, is that of the dog; that is, it is the *less important* of the two wants.

To put it now in more general terms. As we saw, the (necessarily) limited resources at each man's disposal, he, consciously or unconsciously, apportions out among his various wants according to his particular scale, taking care that the more urgent ones are provided for before the less urgent. It is obvious that, in these circumstances, there is a *least* want that is satisfied, although ordinarily we are not conscious what it is. But it immediately comes to the front when, from any cause, our resources are diminished. If a working man's wage is reduced from twenty shillings to nineteen shillings a week, he becomes painfully conscious that some want, hitherto satisfied, must go bare, and the particular want on which he economises immediately points out which was his least, or least urgent, or final want. In this case, all the wants previously satisfied are still satisfied except the last one, and it is proved that none of them depended on having or losing the shilling. Again, all wants under this, just as before, remain unsatisfied whether the shilling is there or not. Only this marginal want is satisfied if the shilling is present and unsatisfied if absent: it alone, then, is the dependent want.

To recur to our illustration. So long as the sailor had the two biscuits, one of them would go to satisfying the higher want (his own), and the other to satisfying the lower want (the dog's), and either biscuit was capable of satisfying either want. But, when one biscuit was lost, the one that remained

not, with the view of acquiring it. As will be seen from above, the two methods of valuation come practically to the same result.

was instantly elevated to satisfying the higher want only: it rose, literally, in value because then it was not a man's *or* a dog's life that depended upon it but a man's only: what was lost was the means of satisfying the *dog's* want: the less important of the two wants was the dependent one; and it is the relation of dependence, as we said, that determines value. We may formulate the proposition thus. The value of a good is measured by the importance of that concrete want which is least urgent among the wants satisfied. And we find that what determines the value of a good is, not its greatest utility, nor its average utility, nor yet its least conceivable utility, but its marginal utility in the given circumstances. Jevons called this the Last or Final Utility. We shall follow Wieser literally in calling it the Marginal Utility. Simple as this proposition is, experience in teaching tells me that it is not easily retained so as to be used. For this reason, it may not be superfluous to confirm its truth by testing it in various circumstances. I cannot improve on Böhm-Bawerk's admirable illustration, and only modify it in non-essential particulars.

A modern Robinson Crusoe has just harvested five sacks of corn. These must be his principal maintenance till next autumn. He disposes of the sacks, according to the scale of his wants, in the following way. One sack he destines for his daily allowance of bread. Another he devotes to cakes, puddings, and the like. He cannot use more than these in eating, so he devotes a third to feeding poultry, and a fourth to the making of a coarse spirit. With these four sacks, we shall say, he is able to satisfy all the wants that occur to him as capable of being directly satisfied by corn, and, having no more pressing use for the fifth sack, he employs it in feeding dogs and cats and other domestic animals, the companions of his lonely life. The question is: What to him is the value of a sack of corn? As before, we ask: What utility will fail him if he lose one sack? It is inconceivable that Crusoe should have any doubt as to his answer: he will, of course, apportion out the sacks that remain as before;—two to food, one to poultry, one to spirits, and he will give up only the feeding of dogs and cats. This is seen to have been the Marginal Utility—the utility on the margin of economic employment or use. What he loses, then, by losing one sack is his former Marginal Utility; and this marginal utility undoubtedly determines the value of a single one of the five sacks. But here we come upon another feature of this valuation. If the marginal utility determines the value of one, it must determine the value of all, as, by hypothesis, all sacks were alike, and therefore all interchangeable. Thus we obtain the universal formula for the valuation of goods in quantity. The value of a quantity of similar goods is the value of the marginal good multiplied by the number of the goods.

To follow the illustration out. If another sack gets lost, the marginal utility is found to have been that of the making of spirits; if still another, the feeding of poultry. Finally, suppose Crusoe to be reduced to the one sack. Then the satisfying of all lesser wants is out of the question; the losing of it means death to him; the marginal utility and the highest utility are one.

Again, suppose Crusoe as merchant bargaining,

say, with the Spaniards. If he have five sacks, he will sell one at a low rate; if he have four, he will ask a higher price; if he have only one, he will not part with it for any money. Extend this to the phenomena of an industrial community. The five sacks represent a larger supply than the four, the four than the three, and so on; and, as the supply decreases, the value of the single sack rises. Now one of the commonest phenomena of a market is that, *ceteris paribus*, increase of supply brings down value and decrease of supply sends it up. To put it in terms of our theory: When the quantity of any good produced is increased, the good is put to lower levels of use; the last want supplied determines the last satisfaction; and this last satisfaction determines the value of all the stock. Here we have the explanation of the old Paradox of Value. If any commodity is available in such quantity that all possible wants for that commodity are supplied, and yet there is a surplus of the commodity, the marginal utility is zero, and the value of the entire stock is nil. And it is also explained how diamonds have a high value compared with bread. The quantity of diamonds available is never sufficient to satisfy more than a fraction of the desire for them: the marginal utility, then, is high. Bread again is, happily, to be had everywhere at a comparatively small expenditure of labour, and the immense supply as compared with the limited wants, puts the marginal utility low.

CHAPTER VI

DIFFICULTIES AND EXPLANATIONS

A CHAPTER may be devoted to answering certain doubts which naturally arise in the reader's mind, and to disentangling some complications which hide the working of our fundamental law.

I. Some goods are perishable, some durable; some are single goods, some are groups of separable elements; and, of these groups again, some are composed of homogeneous, some of very heterogeneous elements. Consequently there is a difference in the way in which goods give off their use, and the marginal utility is not always perfectly obvious.

Thus the first warning we require to take to ourselves is that we must make sure what really is the good we are valuing. In the illustration of last chapter, it was the sack of corn, not the individual grains of corn; it was, that is to say, a group of homogeneous elements considered and valued as a whole. Obviously this is a very different kind of good from, say, a horse or a piano. As durable goods, the latter are, economically, a complex of all the services which they are capable of rendering during their lifetime as goods: their value, therefore, is to be determined by the least use to which their services, one year with another, are put, and not by the least use to which, exceptionally, they are put. Otherwise we should conclude that the utility which a hunting horse may sometimes put forth in drawing a plough, or that which a piano may render at the hands of a schoolgirl, are the marginal utilities determining the value of these goods.

Neglect of this consideration led Schäffle to make the objection that, in desert journeys, the traveller's skin of water, according to our theory, would be measured by the least use to which the water was put: that is to say, the quantity of water employed, say, in washing, would measure the value of the whole skin, while, practically, everybody can see that a good, the possession or non-possession of which meant life or death to the traveller, could not be measured by its washing value. The answer is that here the good which is being valued is the whole water-skin, not the individual drops of water: what measures its value is the amount of well-being that would be lost if the *skin* were lost. If, on the other hand, we were valuing *individual* cubic inches of water in the skin, or if we were valuing *one* skin among many, then Schäffle's calculation would be quite right: that the least use to which the good being valued—the cubic inch or the skin—was put, determined the value of that particular good, the cubic inches or the skin.

Similarly, if we ask what is the value of a water-supply to a city, we are putting a different question from " What is the value of the individual gallon of water ? " The supply, *as a whole*, is the indispensable condition of a collective human want; the unit of valuation here is not the gallon, but the whole supply. So with the value of a mill stream. We must not confound it with the valuelessness of water as drinking water. What the miller values and pays for is the head of water, and on this the individual cups or gallons used for drinking make no difference. Indeed, we have here one of the exceptional cases mentioned in the beginning of last chapter, the valuation of a single good. The water-supply in the above illustrations cannot usually be put alongside of similar supplies and considered as a member of a stock. Its value is measured by the entire utility which it affords.

A more difficult case is presented by the phenomenon of "capitalised value." A quarry or mine which will be worked out in fifty years is valued at a sum much less than the sum of its fifty annual outputs. These annual outputs are seen in a perspective of value diminishing according to their remoteness in time. Say that the first year's output is £100, the second (at an interest rate of 5%) will *now* be worth only £95.23, the third, £90.70, and so on. Adding these together, we obtain a sum which is very much less than £100 × 50, and we express it—conveniently if somewhat misleadingly—by saying that the capital value is so many years' purchase of the annual rent. In other words, to determine the marginal utility of a durable good involves a calculation of the agio on present goods as against future.[1]

II. One must guard against an easy misunderstanding of the expression Lowest Use. Most goods permit of two or more entirely distinct kinds of use:

---

[1] The difficult subjects of capital value and of interest on durable goods are fully treated in Böhm-Bawerk's *Positive Theory of Capital*. See particularly p. 339.

a book, for instance, may be read, or it may be used to light a fire. On the principles just laid down, one might think that it is the latter which determines the value of the book. There are two mistakes here. The first will be seen on referring to the terms of our cardinal proposition. It is the least use to which a good is put, and is, of course, *economically* put, that decides—not the possible uses to which it may be put. If we were valuing two exactly similar copies of one book, and if the *only* uses to which these copies could be put were, to be read or to be burned, then the value of each would be waste-paper value.[1] But this is an almost inconceivable supposition. Books are made to be read, and to enumerate lighting of fires among the possible *uses* of a book is to make the mistake already alluded to—of not being clear as to what is the good that is being valued.

The second and more important mistake is that here we are presenting a case which is essentially different from the typical one given in last chapter. In the case of the peasant we are valuing one of a stock of five similar goods, and concluded that the use to which the fifth sack was put determined the value of the five. In other words, we had a *stock* of goods competing for employment. Now we have employments competing for one good, and, where a good or stock of goods is not sufficient for all possible employments, of course the only economical possibility is that the highest use, and so the highest marginal utility, should decide the value.

[1] Just as the nutritive value of the horse competed with its draught value during the siege of Paris.

III. It follows from what has been said that the value of a good is almost never measured by the utility it actually affords,—its utility to *me*,—but by a foreign utility. In our first illustration of the two biscuits, the utilities actually afforded by the biscuits were, the satisfaction of a man's hunger and the satisfaction of a dog's hunger; but the value of the particular biscuit which actually satisfied the man's hunger was measured by the use of the biscuit to the dog. In modern circumstances, where the existence of money and the presence of stock permit of goods being instantly exchanged for other goods, we can—and do almost unconsciously—change the disposition of our resources so as to shift the loss (which will define our marginal utility) to the least sensitive part.

Suppose that a thrifty housewife has laid in her winter stock of butter, and that by some accident it gets spoiled. Will she be likely to do without butter for the rest of the winter? She will, of course, replace the butter, and do without some comfort or luxury which she would otherwise have allowed herself. That is to say, she will shift the loss to the least sensitive part of her total expenditure. Some part of the total satisfaction must be given up, and this will always be the least in her particular scale. In the circumstances, the satisfaction she now denies herself indicates her least urgent want. Not—be it remembered—her last conceivable want, or her last actually felt want, but the last want that was satisfied when she had the means, or the first that was deprived of its satisfaction when she had to curtail her expenses; in short, the last want satisfied.

Similarly, if I am calculating the loss of value which I suffer from a horse going hopelessly lame, I do not estimate it by the satisfactions of riding and driving I am likely to lose. I replace the horse by economising in other things—perhaps by doing without my summer holiday—and the value of the horse is measured by the "foreign" utility of the summer holiday.

IV. There is a question which naturally rises out of all that has preceded. The value of goods is measured by the lowest, or least, or last use economically made of them :—What determines that this or that particular use is the last? In other words: What determines the *level* of the marginal utility? The answer is ;—the relation existing between a man's wants and the resources or provision he has to meet them. If his wants are few and his resources abundant, the marginal utility will be low, for here all the more urgent wants will be satisfied, and the only wants left to satisfy will be insignificant ones. The value of an additional sovereign to a rich man, for instance, is very small, simply because he has few wants that remain unsatisfied. The same is the case if wants are what we might call "weak"; to the plain liver, the value of the additional sovereign is perhaps as small as to the rich man. If, conversely, a man's wants are many and strong, and his means scanty, the marginal utility will be high, and the sovereign will find wants, and urgent wants, waiting to welcome it. "It comes nearly to the same thing," to quote Böhm-Bawerk, "to say that Usefulness and Scarcity are the ultimate determinants of the value of goods. In so far as the degree of usefulness indicates whether, in its way, the good is capable of more or less important services to human wellbeing, so far does it indicate the height to which the marginal utility, in the most extreme case, *may* rise. But it is the scarcity that decides to what point the marginal utility actually does rise in the concrete case."

CHAPTER VII

COMPLEMENTARY GOODS

As the ultimate goal of economic effort is not the obtaining of goods but the satisfaction of human want, we are not finished with our subject till we have traced the finished good to its end and *raison d'être* in affording this satisfaction. In the present chapter, we have to consider cases where several goods contribute to one satisfaction, and to find what influence this satisfaction has upon their separate values. In such cases the " good " we have to value is, properly speaking, a group, and in the various forms taken by these groups, we meet with some puzzling and far-reaching peculiarities.

The class of Complementary goods, to use Menger's term, is much wider than we are apt to suppose. In consumption goods, it tends to increase with the variety of modern wealth and the development of new tastes. Many of our enjoyments depend on the co-operation of a great many factors, of which usually one is prominent, and the others only assert themselves on rare occasions. Thus the part played by that insignificant commodity, salt, in most of the pleasures of the table, is never appreciated till the want of it—say, at a pic-nic—suggests how indispensable a complement it is. Among productive goods, again, where the division of labour is constantly adding to the number of factors which work together in the making of any good, the complementary character becomes even more apparent. The first thing to be noticed here is that the value of a group, *as a group*, is determined by the marginal utility of the group, not of the separate members. But, as each group may on occasion be broken up, the interesting question is as to the distribution of value among the members, the difference in value between goods as complements and goods as isolated articles.

The simplest case is where the single members of a group are all useless in any other form but that of the group, and are at the same time economically irreplaceable. In valuing boots, for instance, the " good " is the pair ; if I lose one, I lose the entire utility. In such cases—which are, of course, comparatively rare—if I have had the pair and lose one, I lose the entire value of the pair : if I have one and obtain another, I gain the entire value of the pair. Here, then, the value of one single member of the group is the same as the value of the whole group.

This case, however, is really of importance only as introducing the others which follow ; under the assumed conditions we are dealing with a good similar, say, to a pair of compasses or a pair of spectacles, which we can divide into two only at the cost of the whole ; that is to say, it is only externally a group.

A more common form is where the group can afford one utility, and the individual members of it in isolation can afford another but a less utility. Thus the utility of a well-matched pair of roans will be valued at a figure much higher than would be realised by selling the horses separately. Suppose that the utility of the pair is represented by 100, and that of A roan and B roan separately by 50 and 40 : what is the value of A ? To calculate it from the side of the owner : if he has A and B, he has a value of 100 ; if he lose A, he has only B, and B separately has a value of only 40. What he has lost is the difference between 40 and 100. Or, from the side of the buyer : if he gets B he obtains 40 ; if he gets A in addition he obtains 100 ; the value of A, as before, is the difference between 40 and 100. Here, then, A has a different value as complement and as isolated good : in the one case it is worth 60, in the other 50. If we take the case of a well-matched four-in-hand team, we have a more complicated instance of the same ; the whole team makes the most highly valued group, but each pair within that again has a higher group value than the sum of the isolated values which would be attached to each single horse. This case of valuation holds in the very numerous cases where goods are in sets : if we " break the set," the separate members have a less value than they had as complements.

A third case is, where, as before, the group can afford one utility, and the individual members of it separately can afford a less utility, but where some members are replaceable and some are not. In this case, the replaceable members can never obtain any other than the one value : however indispensable they may be to the making of the group, goods that can be easily replaced cannot rise higher than the competition of all other uses allows. Although a load of bricks, for example, were absolutely indispensable to finish the building of a house, the load could never obtain any higher value than that determined by the marginal utility of bricks generally: that is, as determined by all the uses to which bricks generally are put. To the irreplaceable member, on the other hand, falls the remainder of the value of the group. Thus suppose a group A, B, and C, with a group value of 100, and isolated values of 10, 20, 30. If A and B are articles of large manufacture and great demand, while C is a monopoly good, A and B will get 30% of the value, and C the other 70%, although, if the other members were not present in the group, the only value C could realise would be 30.[1]

---

[1] How far the theory of Complementary Goods admits of being applied directly to the problem of distribution of product among the various factors is matter of controversy. Böhm-Bawerk considers that it is the key which will lead to its solution. The line which this suggests would be something like the following. Labour and Capital enter into the composition of all productive groups: in proportion as they are abundant and mobile do they enter into competition with *all* labour and *all* capital, and become perfectly replaceable. In entering into products, then, they can never secure more than their outside value—that fixed by all their employments or uses. The surplus in the price of each product goes to the monopolist factor, whether that monopoly be caused by natural and site advantages of land, mental and technical qualities of undertakers and workers, peculiar conditions of process, or the like. And in proportion as these factors lose their monopoly, does the value of the group shrink; if all the members were to become replaceable, as when first-class land in other countries becomes available through rapid and cheap carriage, or when education makes unskilled labour the exception, the group value, as distinct from the combined isolated values, would disappear.

Wieser, again, considers that this is no more than a valuable suggestion. What guidance, he asks, will this law give where there are several irreplaceable members, and how is the outside value of replaceable members given if not in other combinations of complementary goods which in turn require to be split up into their factors? He points out acutely, in reply to Menger, that, to estimate the proportion contributed by any factor by the loss which would accrue if that factor were absent, is to reckon too much to it, as the loss of a factor from a co-operation will generally disorganise the group and cause more damage than its presence would cause gain. Instead of using the doctrine of Complementary Goods in this way, he proposes to find, by a series of equations, what each factor positively contributes; not, of course, the physical share, but the proportion of value which may be economically " imputed " to it. A great part of the *Natürlicher Werth* is taken up with this doctrine of the " Zurechnung," which is treated in Wieser's usual strong and graphic manner.

CHAPTER VIII

SUBJECTIVE EXCHANGE VALUE

BEFORE passing from subjective or personal value, there remains for consideration one point, which is at once important in itself, and decisive against the old division of the total phenomena under discussion into value in use and value in exchange. To the subtle analysis of Böhm-Bawerk and Wieser we owe the recognition of *subjective* exchange value, as distinct from the purely *objective* exchange value which we have to consider in following chapters. Aristotle said that every good had two uses, "both belonging to the thing as such": similarly we say that every good has two subjective importances, that which it can directly afford, and that which the things got in exchange for it can afford. A little reflection will convince us that subjective value contains these two distinct branches, use value and exchange value.

It may occasionally suit the economist, for purposes of illustration, to discuss the economy of a Crusoe—particularly in problems of production where the essential features of society, as at once a producing and consuming body, are obscured by the division of labour—but, in the simplest form of society known to experience, there is always some barter or exchange of goods. But, wherever this is the case, every good acquires a second possible value as an exchange form of other goods, or a potentiality of obtaining other goods. In the organism called society, each man becomes—at least potentially—richer or poorer with the increase or decrease of its wealth. Some part of our neighbour's goods becomes available for the satisfaction of our want whenever exchange becomes possible between us, inasmuch as the actual existence of his surplus—not to mention his enjoyment of it—depends on our co-operation. Thus the goods which were first valuable to us personally, as possible satisfaction of our want, get a secondary value. Every good becomes potentially a number of other goods, and the range of our possible satisfactions becomes by so much widened. The presence of exchange, in short, gives us a choice of values.

These two kinds of value are possessed in varying degree by different goods. In some, the exchange value may be greater than the use value—as, for instance, when a change in productiveness in the community increases the quantity or improves the quality of things I can get in exchange, while the use value of things I can give in exchange remains unaltered: in others it may be less, as in all cases where habit and association root the goods in our affection. What has to be emphasised is, that the position which every man occupies as a member of society gives to all goods of personal use this other value, and that, as we saw on p. 37, whichever of the two valuations we place higher determines the total subjective value. In other words; there is, as we shall see later, a direct and an indirect satisfaction of wants, corresponding to the division of goods into consumption goods and production goods. Just as grain may be used for bread or for seed, and just as the value of the grain is determined by calculations of marginal utility which take both bread and seed into account as possible uses, so has every good, subjectively considered, a use value and an exchange value, and the total subjective value is calculated on the consideration of both of these as possible uses of the good.

On the other side, there is no doubt that the analysis of exchange value into subjective and objective is subtle, and that it is difficult to keep the two distinct. The real difference may be most easily seen by an illustration. Say that the first edition of *Modern Painters*, which cost me £18 some years ago, now stands in the booksellers' catalogues at £30. It may be assumed that my pleasure, as a cultured man, in the possession of this first edition is measured by something like £30. But suppose I now suffer a reverse of fortune. The subjective use value of the book remains as before: the objective exchange value also remains as before: but the *subjective exchange* value has immensely risen. In my former circumstances the price of £30 was a bagatelle: now it may perhaps pay my insurance premium: this second subjective value is distinct alike from subjective use value and objective exchange value.

In former chapters, we have seen that the value of a good is determined by the marginal utility which depends on it: in the same way this secondary value will be determined by the marginal utility which depends on the things obtained in exchange for the good. This being so, the *amount* of this exchange value will depend on two things : (1) on the objective value, or price, of the goods—which determines what or how many things can be got for them : (2) on the existing state of the owner's want and provision—which determines what place the satisfactions, obtainable from the goods got in exchange, have in his scale of living. For instance : the use to me of the one riding horse which I can just afford may be quite definite, as giving me a pleasant form of exercise. But its subjective *exchange* value depends (1) on the sum of money I could get for him, and (2) what part this sum of money plays in my scale of living.

And here we come in sight of the decisive distinction between subjective and objective exchange value. The objective exchange value of the horse is the same to every one ; the subjective exchange value varies from person to person according to the previous state of his wants and resources. An article in a poor man's house which he can, in case of need, sell for 20/ has a very different importance to him from what a similar article has to a rich man—20/ is a large part of a £50 wage, but a very small proportion of a £1000 income.

The necessity of drawing this distinction lies in the fact that Money has *no* subjective value other than its exchange value. As the tool of exchange the only use to which we can put it is to part with it. It is one of the virtues of a good money that it is never " used," say, as a metal, but passes from hand to hand without question in satisfaction of debt. And yet, as a pound note in a man's pocket is the temporary form of so much bread, meat, lodging, clothes, etc., it is clear that the pound note to the working man has just the marginal utility which these things have. To use Wieser's terse expression : The exchange value of money is the anticipated use value of the things it buys.

CHAPTER IX

FROM SUBJECTIVE TO OBJECTIVE VALUE

Thus far we have considered each man's wants as ranged on a scale; in correspondence with these wants, each man attaches degrees of importance to the goods that come within his knowledge and control, and ranges *goods* also on a similar scale. We have seen that, owing to the infinite subjective differences in men on the one hand, and the effect of provision on the dependence of want on the other, every man's scale is different from every other man's. That is to say, every man, subjectively, attaches his own valuation to goods. As no man, however, liveth to himself, these valuations come together and are compared in every act of barter and exchange. The reflex influence of the valuations that each man meets in any market, however simple, is very great; constant contact of man with man in exchange assimilates the valuations of all, till, unconsciously, we come very much to regard the average valuation made by the people we meet as our own valuation. For instance, in buying an article, if we looked solely and entirely to what that article represented in life, pleasure, satisfaction, self-realisation—however we name our subjective centre—we should, perhaps, value it at 100. But if we meet everywhere with people who value that article, say, from 50 to 60, it is inevitable that our estimate should be strongly affected thereby. And this explains how that, notwithstanding the enormous differences in temperament, culture, and conditions, the valuations which meet on a market do not diverge so widely as one would expect. If we consider that, of three men who bid for a horse, the value of it to A may depend on his being a country doctor, to B, on his being a hunting man, and to C, on his having a sluggish liver, we could scarcely understand how these different values come to be assessed within a few pounds or shillings of each other, if it were not for this kind of arbitrage.

When we say, then, that men who meet as exchangers of different goods put their own subjective valuations on the articles they bring to market, we must be understood to mean valuations that are not more subjective than man himself is. A man's valuations can no more escape being to a great extent the valuations of other men, than he himself can escape being what other people " make " him.

How it comes that each man can compare the importance he attaches to a commodity, as conditioning the satisfaction of want, with the importance of a piece of metal or paper whose only " use " is to pass on, belongs to a department of our science on which, happily, we do not require to enter. It is sufficient for us to say that, in the modern community, we measure " goods in general " by one good, and we grow up so familiarised with the current money scale that no one sees anything strange in valuing, say, a Bible, at thirty pence, or even its author at thirty pieces! In other words, if I enter the market as a buyer for a horse, with the figure of £50 in my mind as the limit of my bid, it is not from a judgment that the horse to me is equal to the satisfaction I could get from fifty gold sovereigns, but from a judgment that the enjoyment or use to be got from the horse is equal to the other personal satisfactions that fifty gold sovereigns represent—to all the current wants of my life which I measure, in my own mind, by that same scale, and count worth £50. The money value is only the universal language in which we express our valuations generally. Thus, through habit and education, it comes that it is more definite and intelligible, either as regards ourselves or others, for us to say that a horse is worth fifty sovereigns, than to say that it is worth so many quarters of corn or hundredweights of iron.

CHAPTER X

PRICE

IN an early chapter, it was said that the one class of objective values which had an interest for economic science was the (purely objective) value in exchange or purchasing power. We escape using this cumbrous expression if we substitute the word Price. The two terms are of course not equivalent: power in exchange is a different thing from the quantum of goods obtained by that power and measuring it: but obviously the two are inseparable, and the laws of the one are the laws of the other. Our present task, then, is the theory of price.[1]

It would, perhaps, not be very difficult to argue that a universal theory of price is impossible. The attempt to base an *entire* economy on the motive of Self-Interest has not been so successful, that many of us are willing to risk the credit of the whole science any longer on an assumption that was never quite true, and is becoming less so as wealth increases and is increasingly spent with a directly moral aim. But,

[1] As might be expected of a reaction against the old position claimed for value in exchange as the sole economic value, the Austrian economists have devoted their energies mainly to the neglected branch, Subjective Value. Böhm-Bawerk alone has followed out the marginal theory of value in detail into the theory of price.

in certain great departments of exchange, if anywhere, the old competitive laws do hold. In stock exchange dealings, in banking, in international transactions, in great organised markets, as iron, wool, cotton, grain, and so on, the egoistic motive is so strongly marked that it is possible to found on it a law which comes, perhaps, as near a scientific law of exchange as we can expect. It may be described as the law of price under perfect competition. It disregards all motives but those of *advantage from the exchange* —always, of course, within the recognised limits of law and respectability. In such markets the "strong" exchanger (buyer or seller) is the one who attaches most importance to the good he wishes to get, and the least importance to the good he gives in exchange—as we can see from the simple consideration that the bidder most likely to carry away a picture from a studio is the one who thinks most of the picture and least of his money, while the artist most likely to clear his stock is the one who thinks least of his pictures and most of the money he will get for them.

The assumptions on which the law is based are the following: that the market is an open and organic one; that buyers and sellers are ordinarily conversant with the conditions of supply and competition; that each party will make an exchange whenever he sees a gain in it; and that he will prefer a greater gain to a less.

They are the assumptions of any ordinary commercial "market."[1] For simplicity's sake, we shall

---

[1] In justice to that large class of economists who strive to suit the stubborn fingers of the economic man to the lute of social life, it may be said that their dislike of the egoistic motive is due simply to its

begin with the simplest possible case, and gradually come to the more complicated.

1st Case. (Isolated Exchange.) A peasant B wishes to buy a horse, and his circumstances are such that he puts the same estimate upon £60 as he does on the possession of a horse. His neighbour S has a horse which he values as worth £20. Here there will certainly be an exchange, as, at a price, say, of £40 both make a gain of £20 over the amount at which, in the worst case, they are willing to exchange. But if the exchangers act on the principle " better a small profit than no exchange," the price may be anything above £20 or under £60, and the actual figure is determined by the " higgling of the market." Here, then, the price will lie between a minimum of the seller's subjective valuation and a maximum of the buyer's subjective valuation.

being egoistic. If struggle and fight is the necessary and healthy condition of industry and commerce, then the utmost demand of the reformer must be a fair field for every one and no favour; if the ethics of commerce are necessarily the ethics of war, we may weep over the fallen but we shall not waste our time crying mercy. But a great many people—and these not the worst economists—think that the economic field may justly be regarded, not as a battle, but as a harvest field, where the greatest results are to be had, not by fighting against, but by working with each other. For the last hundred years, they would say, men have been dazzled by the new possibilities of life which the great increase of wealth has opened up, and the solidarity of mankind has been broken up by the eagerness of each to get hold of an advantage which, obviously, could only be had by the few. Now that the world is passably rich, should we not draw breath, and try to organise the industrial life with an end to the *character* and *conduct* of the workers? Ideas like these have a way of making the egoistic motive seem a little contemptible. But, in justice also to the practical man, it must be said that he ridicules all this mainly because he does not understand that it is a new point of view—the subordination of the economic to the higher life—and because his spiritual advisers have long allowed him to think that the business life has canons of its own, with which " theoretic " morality may not intermeddle.

2d Case. (One-sided competition of Buyers or Sellers.) First, of Buyers. Suppose, instead of one peasant, there are three, B_1 B_2 and B_3, bidding for one horse. B_1 values it at £60: B_2 considers it worth £50: B_3 thinks it worth only £40. Only one can get the horse; but, as S values his horse at £20 only, any of the three buyers may get it. Accordingly they will bid against each other till the figure goes above £40, when B_3 retires from the competition: above £50 B_2 is excluded, and B_1 is left the sole competitor. Then, as in the former case, the price will be fixed somewhere between £60, the subjective valuation of the purchaser, and £50, that of the most capable of the excluded competitors, or, as we should say, between the subjective valuation of the successful and that of the first unsuccessful buyer.

The case of one-sided competition of Sellers is the exact converse of the above.

3d Case. This is the ordinary case of what may be called complete competition—where there are several buyers and several sellers of similar articles. Suppose the case of six buyers each wishing to purchase a barrel of apples, and five sellers each wishing to dispose of one barrel. We assume that the barrels are all of equal quality and offered simultaneously, and that the competitors on both sides know their own interests and follow them.

Buyer 1 values the barrel at and will pay any price under	18/6	Seller 1 values the barrel at and will accept any price above	13/
Buyer 2 ,,	18/	Seller 2 ,,	14/
Buyer 3 ,,	17/6	Seller 3 ,,	15/
Buyer 4 ,,	17/	Seller 4 ,,	16/
Buyer 5 ,,	16/	Seller 5 ,,	17/
Buyer 6 ,,	15/		

Here the subjective valuation which the first three buyers put upon the apples is so high that they are, economically, "capable" of purchasing from any of the sellers. But, naturally, they will not pay more than necessary, and the transaction begins by low offers on the side of the buyers, and holding back on the side of the sellers. Let us follow the course of the bids methodically.

At		Buyers		Sellers
13/6 there are		6 Buyers and		1 Seller
14/	,,	6	,,	1 ,,
14/6	,,	6	,,	2 ,,
15/	,,	5	,,	2 ,,
15/6	,,	5	,,	3 ,,
16/	,,	4	,,	3 ,,
16/1	,,	4	,,	4 ,,
16/6	,,	4	,,	4 ,,
16/11	,,	4	,,	4 ,,
17/	,,	3	,,	4 ,,

Thus we see that, at any price from 16/1 to 16/11, there will be as many buyers as sellers, and the conditions will have emerged at which exchanges take place and price is determined. For, at that price, four buyers and four sellers will make a gain by exchanging. The fourth buyer was willing to pay anything under 17/ and the fourth seller willing to clear anything over 16/; thus both gain by a price which falls between 16/ and 17/, while the three more capable pairs gain proportionally more. And at that price the valuations of the remaining competitors, be they few or many, are unable to have any effect on the exchange. 16/1 will not suit buyers 5 and 6, who are not willing to give more than a maximum of 15/11 and 14/11, and 16/11 will not suit sellers who demand at least 17/1.

Again, any price above 16/11 would cause the fourth buyer to withdraw, and any price under 16/1 would cause the fourth seller to withdraw. The price, then, will be determined somewhere between the subjective valuations of the last buyer and the last seller—what we may call the Marginal Pair.[1] And the most capable exchangers are proved to have been those who put the highest valuation on the commodity they wished (apples or money), and the lowest valuation on the commodity they had (money or apples).

[1] To be exact, this limit may be more closely drawn. Böhm-Bawerk's law is that the price is determined between the valuation of the last buyer and that of the first excluded seller as Higher Limit, and the valuations of the last seller and first excluded buyer as Lower Limit, viz. between the valuations of the Marginal *Pairs*. But, for reasons which will shortly be evident, it is scarcely worth while adding to the difficulty of the subject by too great exactness.

CHAPTER XI

SUBJECTIVE VALUATIONS THE BASIS OF PRICE

It was said in the introductory chapter that we should find Objective Exchange Value to be a superstructure on Subjective Value. The typical scheme in last chapter will abundantly prove this. It is the valuations with which the parties on both sides enter the market that decide;—first, what parties will take part in the competition; second, what is the degree of each party's "capability of exchange"; third, who are the parties that actually come to terms; fourth, who is the last buyer and who the last seller; and fifth, the price. Thus we arrive at Böhm-Bawerk's formal proposition: Price is the resultant of subjective valuations put upon commodity and price-equivalent within a market.

Unless, however, we remember what has been said of the essential nature of value, we shall be apt to stumble over this word "valuation." The price with which a buyer comes to market as the maximum which he is willing to give, does not indicate anything of the absolute amount of wellbeing which the goods he proposes to purchase represent to him. We saw that the subjective value of anything is given by the dependence of a want upon it, and that this dependence is measured by two factors: the want which the good is capable of satisfying and the state of provision already existing to meet that want—in ordinary circumstances, the income or wealth of the valuer. To put it concretely: the valuation of 16/6, which the buyer puts on the barrel of apples in our illustration, is determined by a calculation, first, of the position the fruit takes in his household economy as compared with other forms of food, and, second, of the money figures in which the amount of his income or available wealth enables him to express that position. This, among other things, will explain how two very different classes of competitors may be the " capable " ones ; those whose needs are urgent and those whose resources are plentiful. The valuation of 16/6 may be either the expression of a poor man's necessity, interpreted and limited by the few shillings he can spare from his wages, or the expression of a rich man's whim, measured by the loose money in his pocket.[1]

[1] In connection with this, the following passage is worth attention. "Goods which can only be obtained in very small quantities and which only the rich are likely to demand, will obtain the highest prices. Goods, again, of common quality, suited to the wants of the poor, obtain very low prices, along with those goods of better quality which are so numerous that the poorer classes are able, to a considerable extent, to purchase them. Medium prices, lastly, will rule in the case of goods of which the middle classes are the principal buyers, while poorer people either do not compete or compete only so far as compelled by their most urgent feelings of want. It will readily be understood that changes in the economical provision and power of great classes must be followed by changes in the prices of goods. The greater the inequalities of wealth, the greater will be the differences in price. Luxuries will rise in price as great fortunes increase and fall as they diminish. . . . Thus it is that diamonds and gold stand so very high ; they are luxuries of the rich and richest, and are valued and paid for in the measure of the purchasing power of these classes. Food and iron are at the other end of the scale because they are goods for the people, their value being decided by the valuation and purchasing power of poor men."—Wieser, *Der Natürliche Werth*, pp. 44, 45.

If, then, the subjective valuations on either side do not necessarily say anything of what we might call the absolute worth of things to the valuers, much less does the price which is the resultant of these valuations. It is not even an average of the valuations. However high the valuations of buyers, and however low the valuations of sellers, in an organised market the goods will exchange at the marginal price. And however many be the excluded competitors—the buyers whose subjective valuations do not allow them to buy, and the sellers whose valuations do not allow them to sell, at the marginal price—they are unable to affect the price one way or other.

It should not be necessary to point out that the determination of price in actual life is not the *conscious* resultant of all these valuations. The analysis of price into its factors is as different from the practical synthesis of price as a statue is from an anatomist's plates. The practical man no more knows the machinery set in motion to determine each day's market quotations than the child knows the rules of grammar by which he speaks. It is the same in most economic matters. The theory of money, for instance, is one of the most difficult and complicated parts of economical science, and yet we all grow up with a perfectly definite idea of the relation which a shilling bears to English commodities in general—so definite, indeed, that, when travelling in a country where there is an inconvertible paper currency and where prices are turned upside down by a protective tariff, we do not notice the leap we take when we turn the quarter-dollar note, in our mind, into a silver shilling, and calculate prices on the English basis. In the same way, a business man applies unthinkingly and unerringly all those canons of marginal value and price which we find so puzzling.

But in the business world itself, there is one great simplification of the law of the Marginal Pair. In modern industry, producers do not make for themselves but for the market, and the amount of their own product which they could use in their own consumption is insignificant. Consequently it may almost be said that such goods have no subjective value for the sellers,[1] and we lose one whole side of our valuations. But, on the other hand, this very fact enormously increases the numbers of buyers, and brings their subjective valuations all the closer. Practically, then, our law takes this form: Price is determined by the valuation of the Marginal Buyer.

It will probably be thought that only in the last paragraph have we come to the normal state of things, and so to the only state of things which has any practical interest for us. All the tedious discussion about peasants selling horses, or buyers and sellers wishing to trade for just one barrel of apples each, is beside the mark, it will be said, when we consider that the questions of value which are of importance to us are questions between the innumerable persons who compete with each other in the business of making and buying and selling, and the innumerable persons who buy goods for their own consumption at fixed prices from the shops. The answer to this has already been suggested. As well might we expect to

---

[1] This is not quite true. They have subjective *exchange* value just as money has. The product of labour which has been paid by 20/ of wage has the same sort of subjective value to the wage-payer as the 20/ had. But as the professional producer anticipates demand the subjective value is not so calculable.

understand the organisation of industry by taking our stand on an omnibus in Cheapside, and watching the surging life below, as begin our study of the phenomena of value with the smooth-running machinery of exchange which is the growth of generations. The only way to understand the completed theory of value is to go back to the simplest cases of exchange— perhaps even barter ; find what principles are involved in all exchange ; and then work out the complications and simplifications which come with developed trade. It is impossible to explain the " short cuts " till we know the roundabout road.

It will not have escaped the notice of the critical reader that there are many resemblances between the law now formulated and that known as the law of Supply and Demand. It would be strange if there were not. As in ethics, all theories lead very much to one practical code of morals, so theories of price must all be more or less accurate analyses of the actual transactions of the market. For instance, the zone within the limits of which price is determined is, as we have seen, that lying between the valuations of the Marginal Pair. But every one will have noticed that in this zone supply and demand come, quantitatively, to equilibrium, and hence it is quite correct to say that the market price is found in that zone where supply and demand balance each other.

The resemblance will become clearer if we look at our individual determinants of price. There is—

1st, The Extent of Demand,—that is, the number of people who wish to buy goods because they attach a certain value to them.

2d, The Intensity of Demand,—that is the subjective valuation which these buyers attach to the commodity they wish to obtain, and the subjective valuation of the money they part with.

3*d*, The Extent of Supply,—that is, the number of people who wish to sell goods because they attach a certain value to the money they expect to get in exchange.

4*th*, The Intensity of Supply,—that is, the valuation which these sellers attach to the money they wish to obtain, and which they attach to the commodity they part with.

We shall cease to wonder at resemblances, however, if we remember that our law of value cannot be a rival of any other law which has been recognised as giving, within its sphere, a satisfactory explanation of actual phenomena of value, except in the qualities of breadth of basis or accuracy of details. The impression which most of us, I imagine, have had in relation to the law of Supply and Demand as usually formulated, is that what it says is undeniable, but that it does not say enough. It devotes ample space to the phenomena of supply, but it leaves demand almost entirely without analysis. While it pays lip-service to value as a relative between the two, it gives the impression that the side of supply is so overwhelmingly important that demand may be taken for granted. What the theory which has been developed in the preceding pages does is indeed to make price a resultant of Supply and Demand, but at the same time carefully to analyse these ambiguous expressions, and make price rest finally on subjective valuations of commodities and of price-equivalents made by buyers on the one side and sellers on the other.

CHAPTER XII

COST OF PRODUCTION

WE have now to compare the law of Value at which we have arrived with that most dwelt on by English economists. It is a matter of common experience that, in the case of articles manufactured on a large scale—"freely produced," or reproducible at will—the price always tends towards equality with the cost of their production. On this experience is founded the familiar statement that the value of a good is determined by its cost. Speaking generally, Costs of Production are all the productive goods consumed in the making of a product,—raw and auxiliary materials, machinery, power, and labour. To speak more accurately, we should substitute the term Expenses of Production, thus indicating that the naturally incommensurable "efforts and abstinences" are measured by the money paid for them. On this theory, the value of a good comes from its *past*.

Now, on the theory above explained, we have to show that the causal connection runs the other way, from Product to Cost. Human want, as was shown, is the very first consideration in the Theory of Value. The relation of each man's resources to his varied wants determines what is the last want satisfied in each class of want, and so the

Marginal Utility and subjective value of goods. The figures which buyers and sellers respectively put on their goods determine the competitors, determine the marginal pair or the last buyer, and so determine price. Through price, the subjective valuations are carried back to means of production. As the typical labourer, the peasant, measures the value of his labour by the produce he raises, or the value of his implements by the additional crop they procure, so is all value reflected back from goods to that which makes them. Thus value comes, not from the past of goods but from their future; that is to say, from the side of consumption in satisfying want. Goods stand midway between production and consumption. In the old reading it was the former term that gave value: in the new, it is the latter.

Before going further, it is necessary more exactly to define the connection between production and consumption goods.

All goods find their goal in satisfying the want of man. As Roscher finely says, *Ausgangspunkt, wie Zielpunkt unserer Wissenschaft ist der Mensch.* The consumption-good then—the good which is to find its destiny, and its life-work, in ministering to human want—is that for which and towards which we set in motion the whole machinery of industry. From the soil or the mine downward, every productive instrument is, economically, a consumption-good *in the making.* This Menger has put in terms which are now classical. He calls consumption-goods, goods of the first or lowest rank. The goods which co-operate in immediately producing these—the group of productive instruments used in the last stage of production —he calls goods of second rank. The factors of this second group, again, are goods of third rank, and so on. Thus, if a loaf is the consumption-good or the good of first rank, the flour, the oven, and the baker's labour form the group of second rank; the wheat, the mill, the labour, and the material that makes the oven, the group of third rank; the land, the agricultural implements, the materials of the mill, etc., the group of fourth rank, and so on. Now, as we have seen, consumption-goods receive their value from the dependence of some want upon them—from their being the condition of some satisfaction. Take, then, the good, a loaf of bread. The value of the loaf in the baker's shop is determined subjectively by its marginal utility to the consumers, and the valuations (based on this marginal utility) of buyers and sellers decide the market price at which the bread is put on the market. Looking back now at the continuity of production and consumption goods, we see that the last group of productive goods which issues in the bread is really the *loaf in the making*. If the baker had not that group he would not have the bread, and we should lose our marginal utility—the satisfaction of the want. What, then, depends on the having or losing the group of second rank? Simply the marginal utility of the finished good. Tracing back the loaf to more and more remote groups, we find, similarly, that what depends upon them all is, at different points of time, the marginal utility of the finished consumption-good: that is to say, they are all, economically, the loaf in the making. In short, value depends on a relation to human wellbeing as indicated by the satisfaction of want; and productive goods only come into contact with human wellbeing through the final member of the chain, the consumption-good. No one values the iron ore, or the ragged " pig," for what it is in itself. Ingenious and delicate as may be the machine, no one puts together these cunning arrangements of wheels and pulleys and rollers for the sake of showing the machinist's skill, or the working of mechanical powers. Even the smooth and gossamer yarn is not a thing which can satisfy any human want. All these goods are only " good " because they are cloth, or some other consumption-good, in the making. We " value " them, not because we see the iron fabrics passing, by wear and tear of the machine, into the warp, or the threads of human life being woven into the weft, but because, with prophetic eyes, we see the web covering the otherwise bare backs of men and women, and giving up its life in ministering to theirs.

The conduction of value, then, would seem to be, from product [1] to means of production; and this would, probably, be generally recognised if every product were connected immediately with only one group of means of production. In the case of a wine grower it is easy enough to see that the value of the grapes is derived from the wine, and the value of the vineyard from the grapes; that the price, for instance, at which he would let his land to a third party, or the number of labourers he could, economically, hire to assist him, is determined by average productiveness. Or suppose we value a good subjectively, say, at £100, there seems a very good reason why we should be willing to pay, say, £50 for the labour of raising raw material, £40 for

---

[1] It need scarcely be said that it is *anticipated* product: in modern circumstances it is of course impossible for the fore producers to wait on final sales, even if makers and merchants did not regularly anticipate demand; but this does not affect the logical connection.

manufacturing it, and £10 for delivering it. But in modern divided industry it is, of course, impossible for most of the intermediate producers to know anything about the marginal utility, or the price which the goods will obtain when finished. The labourer paid 20/ a week for lumbering will scarcely connect his wage with the price of the delicately carved cabinet which, among other final products, is the ultimate goal of his labour. Even the timber merchant, as a rule, will not make his calculations of the price he can pay for wood with any better knowledge of its final destiny. But each branch of production has an immediate product as well as an ultimate one, and, in the marginal utility and price of this intermediate product, it finds its value and price. Thus though the conduction of value from anticipated final product back to intermediate product, and from that back to the very first product of all, may remain hidden from each and every producer, the organisation of industry practically carries the information from stage to stage. The weaver finds a market value already attached to yarn, and, measuring by that, he puts a value upon his labour and the raw material for which he offers. But the cloth he weaves is the means of production for the next intermediate product, and gets its value from it again. And so the line of communication goes on down the ranks till it comes to the final consumption-good.

The proof of this conduction is not far to seek: it is found in the common phenomenon of Dead Stock. However great the cost expended on an article, if the public will not have it, all the costs in Christendom will not give it a value; and, if the good continues "dead," all the machinery and buildings by which it would have been made lose their value, except in as far as they can be turned to other uses, and get another value from another product. Even labour suffers. Whatever the expense of his special training, the labourer can give no value to his work, and loses his wage to the extent that he cannot adapt his skill to other employments. Suppose that an article of which there is a stock, goes out of fashion, the value and the price of it fall at once. The first thing the immediate manufacturer does is to ask himself if he can reduce his costs to suit the new price: if he cannot, he abandons the manufacture, and it passes probably to some man who is able to produce more cheaply, it may be by reducing wages and salaries, by new processes and more complicated machinery, or, perhaps, by employing women instead of men. In any case the cost must conform to the value.

A striking proof of this is given in the case of silver. Most people have a dim idea that silver, as one of the precious metals, has a value almost innate. Yet after 1873 mine after mine was abandoned although the ores were as rich and the reefs as plentiful as ever. What was the cause?—Simply that silver was discarded as currency in certain countries: that is to say, silver fell in the estimation of great communities, and the loss of value was carried back till the price realised by the virgin silver was not enough to pay for the mining of it.

Of course the identity of value between final product and groups of higher and higher rank is not absolute. It would be strange if it were; for where all the groups get their value from the last product, and this gets its value from a thing so inconstant as human want and so elastic as human provision, it is to be expected that the calculation which conducts value back and back, will, often enough, be mistaken. Builders tempted, by high freights at a time of sudden demand, to lay down a ship, must reckon with the possibility that, ere it be finished, the tide of prosperity may have ebbed, and that the price realised for the ship may scarce repay the wages and prices paid in anticipation. And, besides these fluctuations which cannot be reduced to law, and are often the chances on which the employer (as distinguished from the capitalist) makes his great profits—and losses—there is one constant difference between the value of the productive groups and that of the final product; that is, Interest. With this, however, we have no concern here.

CHAPTER XIII

FROM MARGINAL PRODUCTS TO COST OF PRODUCTION

THUS far the matter has been comparatively simple. We have looked at a concatenation of successive groups with one final product, and with, of course, one marginal utility and one value. But we have now to face the fact that productive groups may pass into a great number of final products, each with a different marginal utility and value. The more industry is divided, the more is this the case. Productive goods, such as coal, oil, labour, go more or less to the making of millions of products. It is this that gives the Supply side its almost overwhelming weight in modern economic science. And it is here that we find the *raison d'être* of the law of cost as a convenient abbreviated expression of a deeper law. Let us follow the matter out methodically.

A stock of productive goods, which we shall call X, is capable of producing finished products A, B, and C. The value of these products for the time is, respectively, 100, 110, and 120. Which product will determine the value of the productive unit of X?—It will be the least of the three. For, suppose so many units of the stock X get lost that it is impossible to make A, B, *and* C, the one given up will, of course, be A,—the employment of X which produces the least valuable product. Any other choice would be contrary to economic conduct. When we say, then, that means of production get their value from their product, we must be understood as meaning the value of their final or Marginal Product.

But, again, if B and C are articles of large common manufacture, they cannot long retain their value of 110 and 120; it is merely a question of time till their value falls to 100. Here we begin to see the plausibility of the idea that cost of production determines value.

To put this concretely. A man has a farm of 90 acres divided among three crops, which, in the circumstances of the market, give him three different returns. On 30 acres, he grows wheat, which, we shall suppose, yields him a value represented by 100; on another 30 acres, he grows potatoes, which yield him, say, 110; on another 30 acres, he grows barley, which yields him 120. What is the value of the productive group made up of his labour and one third of his land? (We leave out of account, for simplicity's sake, the other co-operating factors.) If the value were given to land and labour by the *actual* returns there would be three different values, and this really is the case where competition has not its full play. But, if there is no monopolist factor, these three values cannot be maintained. The value of the first product, 100, determines the value of the means of production, the labour and land, and it is only a question of time and competition till this value of the means of production has imposed itself on the potatoes and the barley, and reduced their price to the same comparative level as that of wheat.

Here, then, we have the explanation of the law of cost of production. It is quite true that, in the case of goods reproducible at will, or, in our vocabulary, in cases where substitutes are immediately available either by exchange or from production, the costs of production determine the value, and the formula is both true and convenient. All the same, it is merely a particular instance of the universal law of Marginal Utility. In all cases, the marginal utility of the last product economically produced determines the value of the means of production; these means of production then become the intermediate standard; and the value of goods produced from them cannot, in the long run, be higher than the value got from the marginal product.

The practical working of the law may be seen from a personal experience of the writer. In the cotton thread trade, there was for years a demand for a thread which should be a fair substitute for the much more expensive article, sewing silk. The prices of cotton thread and of silk thread respectively gave housewives and shopkeepers a rough guide to a subjective valuation, and the figure put upon this demand was something like 20/. (It could not be more for the reason that no cotton substitute was able to take the place of silk in any but a few of its least important uses.) This price, offered by shopkeepers to travellers, told the cotton-thread manufacturers what they could offer to cotton spinners for superior yarns, and what they could afford for more expensive chemicals and polishing machinery. As consequence, after many experiments the silk substitute was produced, and sent into the market at a price of 20/. But once those superior yarns were made, the cotton spinners, increasing the production of them, found other outlets. Before long the thread makers saw that this silk substitute was not the *marginal* product of those particular yarns : that, in fact, other cotton threads of lower price were being made from the same yarns. These yarns then entered into the cost of silk substitute with the predetermined lower value given them by the other finished goods, and, in a short time, the price of the silk substitute fell from 20/ to 18/, in conformity with the value put upon the yarns by the new marginal product. The same phenomenon occurs whenever a demand for a new article or a modification of an old one arises, and is interpreted by the enterprise of manufacturers.

CHAPTER XIV

FROM COST OF PRODUCTION TO PRODUCT

If, finally, we take the case of those most many-sided productive goods, Iron and Labour, the proof of our theory may be considered fully tested.

Leaving out complementary factors, which do not disturb the action of the law and would complicate our statement, suppose that iron is the sole productive good in the making of those various iron wares we find selling at different prices in the ironmongers' shops. The general opinion is that it is the price of iron—disregarding other factors—that determines the price of iron wares, from nails to kitchen ranges. And what we have to prove is that the conduction of value really runs in the opposite direction—from nails and ranges to raw iron.

Suppose for the moment that the prices obtainable for these products range from 40/ to 48/ for a given unit. That is to say: the ton of iron, when manufactured into, say, nails fetches 40/, when manufactured into other articles, it fetches respectively 42/, 44/, 46/, 48/. These prices are the result of the condition of the market at the moment. The manufacturers of these products—we shall call them respectively A, B, C, D, and E—represent the demand for iron, and the price they will be able to offer for iron depends on the prices obtained by these articles.

On the other hand, the supply of raw iron held in store will naturally pass to the most capable buyers—the most capable manufacturers of iron wares—at the valuation of the last buyer. Suppose the stocks of iron are sufficient to meet the demand of E, D, and C, the valuation of C, the last buyer, will determine the price of iron at 44/ per ton. So far all has gone to show that it is the iron wares—through the marginal product—which determine the price of the productive good, iron.

But now we come to a feature which gives countenance to the old theory. So long as the prices of iron wares—always assuming that iron is the sole productive group employed in the manufacture—range from 40/ to 48/, while the market price of iron stands at 44/, it is a proof that competition has not done its work. What naturally follows? Producers D and E who are getting respectively 2/ and 4/ advantage over costs will increase the output of their particular iron wares till over-supply brings down the price to 44/. On the other hand, producers A and B, who get respectively 4/ and 2/ less than cost, will curtail their production, till decrease of supply raises their prices to 44/. Thus, from above and from below, competition is always levelling prices to the cost of production. Here it is quite true that cost of production imposes itself on product. What is forgotten is that the cost of production is itself first determined by the marginal product.

There is, however, a stronger argument for the old theory. Stocks of iron are not a fixed quantity. If new and productive mines are opened, or new processes discovered, the supply of iron increases, and prices of all iron products will certainly fall. Does this not prove that the value of iron wares is regulated by the cost of producing iron?

Here we have a difficult subject to disentangle, and it will be as well to simplify it. Suppose a farmer is supplying a small village with potatoes, and by a new method of cultivation manages to double his crop for the former expenses of labour. What will happen as regards the price of potatoes? From our knowledge of what competition does in large production we are apt to say: " prices of potatoes will fall 50%." This may be the final result, but not necessarily so, and at any rate the movement of price is instructive. The farmer is now able to sell at half the price if he wishes, but it is his interest to keep up the price as long as he can. What, however, will certainly happen, in normal circumstances, is that he will increase his production of potatoes. But it is not the case that, whatever nature and man produce, men will desire: it is, rather, that what man desires he usually sets nature and men to produce. To take off the extra supply of potatoes, then, the farmer must find a wider circle of demand than before; but there is nothing to lead us to suppose that there is any wider circle of demand at the old price. What we may safely suppose is that a great many housewives will buy extra potatoes if they can get them cheaper, but, in any case, the decision lies absolutely with them whether they will take more or not. It is easy to fall into the mistake of thinking that there will be a demand for everything produced if it is sold at a reasonable price, but this idea simply arises from the fact that producers anticipate desire and tempt demand. In the present case, demand must come from some level of want which was not satisfied at the former price, and is ready waiting to take up the extra supply if the price is brought down.

If, however, as may very well happen—not in the case of potatoes probably, but in large articles of limited consumption—there is no such circle of demand at lower levels, what will happen is that the farmer will dismiss half the hired labour, produce the same quantity of potatoes as before, and maintain the former high price. For farmers, like other business men, do not put themselves on "salaries," and give the public the benefit of all cheapening of production. It is characteristic of the capitalist employer in all departments that he speculates on having a profit, and thinks no profit too high, just because, as a speculative gain, it may be balanced any year by as great a loss. It is contrary, then, to all experience to think that employers will voluntarily reduce prices —any more than they will voluntarily raise wage or pay higher interest—because costs have decreased. They only do so under the compulsion of fear that their rivals will cut the feet from under them. Where competition is active, it will often seem as if reduction of costs were almost immediately followed by fall in prices of products; but, in the last resort— and that is what concerns us in seeking for a universal law of value—the new prices are determined by the lower and wider levels of want which are ready to take up increased supply of the majority of ordinary commodities.

Transfer the argument now to the production of iron. If new mines are opened, the first phenomenon is not a fall in the price of iron, but an increase of supply. If the demand from the side of iron wares has hitherto been met at the price—as we must assume—the new extra supply will not be taken off at the price, and there is, for the moment, over-supply. At this point, the lower level of demand for iron wares hitherto unsatisfied asserts itself, and offers its subjective valuation. This is accepted: a new marginal employment is found for iron. The price of this marginal product now determines the price of the productive good iron; and in time it is possible for competition to impose this marginal value on all iron products, and the price of iron wares generally falls.

Lastly, take the case of Labour. Here we have a productive good of the same nature as iron in that it is capable of employment in an infinite number of ways. The labouring power of a nation, like all its other productive goods, goes steadily into the most remunerative employments one after another. But, of all productive goods, labour shows most evidently that it has no predetermined value, but gets its value entirely from what it produces. Consequently, the price of labour is, naturally, as variable as the price of its products. Some products of labour will for the time fetch a price equal to 10/ a day of wage; others, prices equal to 9/; and so on down the scale, perhaps, to 3/ per day. If the available labour as a whole is taken up at that wage, those products of labour which pay 3/ per day of price to labour will assert themselves as the marginal products, and that wage will seem in its turn to determine the value of other products. But if population goes on increasing, other things remaining the same, and a new supply of labour comes forward, this labour will inevitably seek lower levels of demand—for, of all goods, labour is the one that will not "keep." On the other hand, there are at any time endless wants waiting on satisfaction, but not able to pay the marginal cost of satisfaction, the 3/ per day. Consequently, as buyers with a lower valuation than the marginal one, they do not affect price. But now the new surplus supply of labour and the unsatisfied layer of wants come together. Labour is set to satisfy wants that offer, say, 2/6 per day of wage for their satisfaction, and the products thus resulting become the marginal products. Happily for the labourer, competition cannot do its perfect work where the commodity bought and sold is human life: but, if labour were entirely mobile, it would only be a question of time till the marginal product fixed the wage of labour generally, and wages fell in harmony with the new marginal costs—the low wage for what the labourers produced being, let us hope, more than recouped by the universal fall in prices of what the labourers consumed.

CHAPTER XV

CONCLUSION

Thus we have found that what determines the value of productive goods where the product is one single good directly connected with them, and what determines it in the most complicated cases, where the conduction of value is, first, to means of production, and, then, back again to product, is always the marginal utility, the utility of the marginal product. As the vineyards of Tokay get their value from the wine of their grapes, and as cotton gets its value from the bare backs it covers, so do iron, coal, and labour get their value in the last resort—far as may be the course from post to finish—from the last employment into which they enter.

It has already been said that the law developed in the previous chapters is not a rival to that which makes value determined by the relations of Supply and Demand, but a more adequate expression of it. So, in the last three chapters, the emphasis necessary to prove a difficult proposition may have given the impression that the present law is put forward in contradiction of the determination of price, in the great majority of cases, by costs of production. It may, then, be as well to remember that the work of the Austrian school is a quest for the *fundamental* law of value. In the complicated circumstances of modern industry, it is not easy to see the real nexus of cause and effect. In a developed market, where production speculates on demand, value naturally assumes the appearance of being determined beforehand. Human wants are tempted, as it were, instead of giving the initiative. Thus the impression is easily got, and with difficulty got rid of, that human want will pay the price which production dictates, the fact being that production must, in the long run, conform to the nature and measure of human want. And thus also, I am afraid, comes the idea, certainly common among the employing classes, that wages are dictated by them from above, instead of being produced by the labourers themselves—an idea degenerating in many cases into the belief that combinations of workers to secure their share in the product are illegitimate interferences with capital.

What is contended is that the Law of Cost is a good working secondary law as regards articles reproducible at will under large and organised production; that is, of course, as regards the vast majority of goods produced. But it has always been taught by economists that it did not hold outside these cases. On the other hand, the Law of Marginal Utility is claimed as the universal and fundamental law of value. It has not been difficult to prove its validity in the simpler cases; and if now, in the later chapters, our law has been shown to be the real background of the empirical Law of Cost, the contention is justified.

And thus, as representing, however humbly, the modern Austrian school, I may close with the words written by our own Jevons twenty years ago.

"Repeated reflection and inquiry have led me to the somewhat novel opinion, that *value depends entirely upon utility*. Prevailing opinions make labour rather than utility the origin of value; and there are even those who distinctly assert that labour is the *cause* of value. I show, on the contrary, that we have only to trace out carefully the natural laws of the variation of utility, as depending upon the quantity of commodity in our possession, in order to arrive at a satisfactory theory of exchange, of which the ordinary laws of supply and demand are a necessary consequence. This theory is in harmony with facts; and, whenever there is any apparent reason for the belief that labour is the cause of value, we obtain an explanation of the reason. Labour is found often to determine value, but only in an indirect manner, by varying the degree of utility of the commodity through an increase or limitation of the supply."

APPENDIX I

WIESER'S chapter on the paradox of value (*Natürlicher Werth*, i. §§ 7 and 10) deserves more space than could appropriately be given it in the text. I therefore give the substance of it here. Suppose, he says, that I have a certain good the employment of which yields me a utility represented by 10, and that I add successively 10 similar goods to my stock, the marginal utility, at each addition diminishing by 1. The value of the stock will stand successively at 10, 18 (9 × 2), 24 (8 × 3), 28 (7 × 4), 30 (6 × 5), 30 (5 × 6), 28 (4 × 7), 24 (3 × 8), 18 (2 × 9), 10 (1 × 10), 0 (0 × 11). Here, obviously, each added good brings a smaller utility than the last, and at each addition the marginal utility, and with it the value, of the unit of goods falls. But while the value of the single good thus steadily falls, the value of the whole stock describes a peculiar course: it rises from 10 to 30, pauses there a moment, and then falls from 30 to zero. This phenomenon of increasing wealth accompanied by decreasing value is a paradox from which we shall not escape so long as we consider value a simple and positive amount. Value arises in the combination of two elements, a positive and a negative. It is a combined amount, or, more accurately, a residual amount. The positive element in value is the gratification from the use of goods. This gratification is subject to a natural law of "diminishing returns": as the first draught of any pleasure is the most grateful, and as the gratification weakens at every repetition, so a single good stands highest in our estimation, and each addition to the stock occupies a lower place. The value of the stock successively may be represented thus—

When the stock consists of	1	2	3	4	5	6	7	8	9	10	11	goods,
the total gratification is	10	19	27	34	40	45	49	52	54	55	55	units.

This would be the movement of value if value were simply positive: beyond a certain point, additions to the stock would *add* no value, but they would not cause any *loss* of value, and the highest point would come last in the series. But there is another, and a negative element in value.

It arises from the indifference which we naturally feel towards goods. To man only the human is really important: by nature his thought, his sympathy is for himself; for *things* he only cares, in the first instance, as he finds in them any relation to human interests. This interest may take the form of sympathy with pain or pleasure in the animal world; or that of religious and poetic feeling suggesting the unity of all life; or, lastly, that of economic valuation finding in things the auxiliaries and conditions of human wellbeing. This natural indifference is so great that it requires a peculiar compulsion before we look at anything outside us as having importance or value. Simple utility is not enough: if useful things are present in superfluity, we think no more of them than we do of the sand on the sea shore. It is only when our wellbeing is not assured that an interest awakens in the things on which it is seen to depend, and that we exert ourselves to acquire these things. The overcoming of this natural resistance, then, is something with which we have to reckon. The greater our need, the less the resistance: in cases of extreme need, it disappears altogether, and we identify our fate with the fate of the goods which " are life or death to us." The resistance is at its height when we have everything in excess, and feel no thanks due to goods which cannot help ministering to our enjoyment—for there is no reason why we should value additional goods unless they give us additional well-being. Between these two extremes, the interest we transfer to goods is proportioned to the interest we take in what they do for us. But we do not attach to them the whole of the interest they really have for us: we do not require to do so, for goods of a stock are not estimated according to their actual importance, but according to the marginal utility they afford. All utility over the marginal utility is kept back from the value of the goods, and this gives us the figures for the strength of the resistance: the negative element is equal to the surplus value deducted. Thus, when the stock consists of two goods, the actual gratification is $10+9=19$, while the calculation of the value is $9 \times 2 = 18$, leaving a surplus of 1: when the stock consists of 4 the actual gratification is $10+9+8+7=34$, but the value is $7 \times 4 = 28$, leaving a surplus of 6, and so on. Putting these two scales together we have the following—

	1	2	3	4	5	6	7	8	9	10	11
Positive (+)	$\frac{1}{10}$	$\frac{2}{19}$	$\frac{3}{27}$	$\frac{4}{34}$	$\frac{5}{40}$	$\frac{6}{45}$	$\frac{7}{49}$	$\frac{8}{52}$	$\frac{9}{54}$	$\frac{10}{55}$	$\frac{11}{55}$
Negative (−)	0	1	3	6	10	15	21	28	36	45	55
Residual (+)	10	18	24	28	30	30	28	24	18	10	0

That is to say, combining the positive and the negative elements, we get Residual Amounts corresponding to the marginal scale. Thus we see that the value of a stock increases with the increase of its units so long as the positive element is in the ascendant: *i.e.* so long as the increment of value obtained from the newly-acquired good is greater than the decrement of value which its addition causes to every good already in the stock. We may call this the "Up Grade" of the movement of value. On the other hand, the value of a stock falls in the converse circumstances, and this marks the "Down Grade" of value. Twice, then, in the development of value is zero touched—when we have nothing and when we have all: in the former case, because value has no object to which to attach; in the latter, because there is no subjective motive to attach it to anything. In practical life, we have mostly to do with the up grade of value. In most of our possessions, we are so far from superfluity that increase of quantity involves increase of value; while the individual value of the single good sinks, that of the stock rises. And this is the reason why we usually measure wealth and riches by the sum of the values of their elements, and count it hard if the value of our property and our returns goes down. And this, again, is why it seems paradoxical when we find that the amount of goods and enjoyment of wealth and welfare has increased while their "value" has gone down. It does on rare occasions happen that individual branches of economy are for the moment forced on to the down grade—as in the case of phenomenal weather producing a miraculous crop, or the discovery of new mineral strata of unsuspected richness, or great discoveries in machinery and processes, or, perhaps, the fact of producers extending too fast from overreaching greed or foolish overestimate of demand. But it is probable that the conditions of industry, as a whole, will never be favourable enough to bring production so near excess that the down grade of value will be permanently entered on. All the same, the existence of what we call the "free gifts of nature" allows us no room to doubt that value disappears whenever superfluity is reached, and this gives us the best confirmation of the statement that it must decrease as we come near it

APPENDIX II

THEORY OF VALUE: THE DEMAND SIDE

MANY of the difficulties in the Theory of Value arise from not keeping clearly before us that it is a Theory of Human Valuation; of the values which men do—not of what they should—put on things. The idea of "intrinsic value" dies hard.

Connection with Wealth.—" Wealth consists of useful things." "Wealth consists of valuable things." Both statements reflect current views, and both are true, the one suggesting an Inventory, the other a Calculation of the same things.

The Problem stated.—Twenty goods, different in substance, size, shape, quality, use, are equal in this, that a twenty-first good, say a shilling, will purchase any of them. What is it that puts them in a balance, and pronounces all the twenty-one goods equal in value?

An Indication.—It has been suggested that Value is the order of our Preferences. But can one thing, strictly speaking, be "preferred" to another unless the two are at equal price? At any rate, it cannot be said *simpliciter* that the ordinary man "prefers" diamonds to his dinner. The suggestion, however, reminds us that we never value anything by itself; we always value it by reference to something else. Thus, in the last resort, Value expresses an order—a more or less.

Comparison with other Measures.—Measures do not hang

in the air; they are based on something—a unit proclaimed by Governments, either quite arbitrarily or as corresponding to some presumably fixed natural phenomenon, *e.g.*, the yard and the metre. So, in ancient times, the gold talent *weighed* 120 to 140 food-grains, and was equated, by convention, to the ox, which was the primitive unit of value. But this throws no light on the *value* measurement which equated the ox to the talent. (It is submitted, in passing, that the equation was only an ideal one—a convenient point of departure; that the ox generally exchanged for the talent with a plus or a minus, just as the point of departure for a lawyer's fee is "six and eightpence," or as the 30 acres presumed necessary for the support of a manorial family was the point of departure for a "virgate.") The grain basis of the gold talent, however, suggests that the value measurement also has a natural basis;—that Value is the comparison and expression of things in a Common Third. What is this Common Third?

Labour as the Common Third.—A famous theory says that value expresses and measures the more or less of labour " embodied " in goods—the labour involved in the getting or making of goods. This, however, involves the idea of a Unit of Labour, *i.e.*, it assumes the possibility of bringing all labour to a common expression—a previous equation. This difficulty seems insuperable, even when we look only at one side of the primitive equation: can any labour be more different in amount, intensity, and quality than that which gets gold? Suppose this overcome, and suppose the similar difficulty of equating the various labours involved in getting oxen overcome, what common quality measures these two sets of labours? When, finally, one tries to weigh head labour against hand labour, *except by the price paid for their results*, the full impossibility stands revealed. But, of course, to bring different labours to an equality by referring to the price paid for their results, is to beg the whole question. Assume that things are valuable and variously valuable, and one may pronounce that the labour spent on them will be correspondingly valuable; but the previous question is—Why are the products so variously valued? The hold which the Labour Theory took in last century can be explained only by its introduction of a moral idea making results (prices) depend on that which makes and elevates man, namely, Labour. But it certainly would make Value something very different from Human Valuation. (Note in passing that this theory is not to be confounded with the Cost of Production theory, which, indeed, is the other—the Supply—side of the true theory.)

Life as the Common Third.—When Adam Smith said that water had great value in use, and diamonds scarcely any, he suggested life as the common third. It might, indeed, be possible to draw out a "natural order" of values—a hierarchy of things according to their power of sustaining an average human life. An animal or a Crusoe might value things in this way. It is evident that in prehistoric times the ox was adopted as the standard because of its measurable potentiality in this respect. But, in any community that we know, "life" is too complex to afford a basis; not only does "living" become intellectual, moral, æsthetic, but goods naturally availing to life, becoming plentiful, notoriously lose their value. This, however, suggests the true answer.

Utility as the Common Third.—The common third is Utility. Jevons' words, in his introduction to the *Theory of Political Economy* (1871) put this succinctly. "Repeated reflection and inquiry have led me to the somewhat novel opinion that *Value depends entirely upon Utility.* Prevailing opinions make Labour rather than Utility the origin of value; and there are even those who distinctly assert that Labour is the *cause* of Value. I show, on the contrary, that we have only to trace out carefully the natural laws of the variation of Utility, as depending upon the quantity of commodity in our possession, to arrive at a satisfactory theory of exchange, of which the ordinary laws of supply and demand are a necessary consequence. This theory is in harmony with facts; and, whenever there is any apparent reason for the belief that Labour is the cause of Value, we obtain an explanation of the reason. Labour is found often to determine Value, but only in an indirect manner, by varying the degree of Utility of the commodity through an increase or limitation of the supply." Here, however, we must hark back to first principles, and see what we mean by Utility. The question is pertinent, not only because of the misleading meaning given to the word by current opinion, but because of its association with the supposed materialist tendencies of Utilitarianism—an association, indeed, from which economic science still suffers.

The Boundary Line in Economics.—Every science, as expressing the division of labour which rules in thought as in industry, must limit itself and specialise. Granting in the fullest way that men never escape the obligation to ethical conduct in the industrial as in the political life, there can be nothing but confusion if we do not draw a line, however arbitrary, between ethical science and economic science, just as we draw a line between ethical science and political science. Let us drop, so far as possible, the word Wellbeing, which is generally taken as explaining " Wealth," and has, in current language and in cruder economics, become confused with it. Take it from Aristotle that Happiness is the " end in itself "—the Good for which we desire all other things. Men, blindly seeking Happiness, aim, not indeed at Money, but at the things which Money can buy, and these they call Wealth. It is true that many of these things are as aptly called Illth (Ruskin's word), still the "Illth" is not in themselves, but in the uses men make of them. They are, at any rate, "goods," and they often prove themselves "good" by finding their other uses. What remains beyond doubt is that men buy goods—that is, express and measure the value they attach to them in a money price—because they *want* them. Why do they want them? We may avoid the ethical connotation of the word Happiness by taking a word which has been hypothecated by economics, and saying that they seek Satisfaction. Here "Wealth" becomes marked out, both currently and scientifically, as the "collection of instruments" which aims, rightly or wrongly, at this Satisfaction. We take Satisfaction, then, as the boundary line of Economics—although a limit always suggests something on the further side. But what is Satisfaction?

Satisfaction.—Satisfaction is found in men and animals alike, in the filling of physical wants and the forth-putting of activities. To these man adds infinite desires—less urgent, perhaps, but hungrier and more far-reaching than physical wants. Mark, however, that wants, desires, and activities merge into one another—human hunger, *e.g.*, is appetite; the best life is one long purposed activity, subordinating, but necessitating, the satisfaction of wants and desires incidental to it.

Goods.—This satisfaction gives us the meaning of Goods. The reason—and the sole reason—why we want goods is that by our constitution we cannot get satisfaction without them. Wealth, then, is the complex of goods on which satisfaction is presumed to be dependent.

Law of Satiable Wants.—All wants and desires weaken with satisfaction, and, if satisfaction is carried far enough, they, for the moment, disappear. Generally, however, as our wants and desires are many and various, and as one satisfaction limits another, we leave off in the satisfaction of any want at a margin far short of satiation. This is purely a physiological and psychological phenomenon, not an economic law.

Law of Diminishing Utility.—Satisfactions being dependent on Goods, we easily reflect the satisfaction on to the goods, and use the relative word Utility as if it were a quality of goods. Transferring, by the same process, the weakening satisfactions to goods successively presented to a want (or to similar goods in our possession), we get a statement of a fundamental tendency of human nature, the Law of Diminishing Utility; namely, that the additional utility which a person attaches to a given increase of his stock of anything diminishes as the stock increases. This is purely an Economic Law; for, physically considered, the goods themselves retain their material content unchanged, and are not in the abstract less capable of satisfying want, *if there be want*. Thus is explained Jevons' "variation of Utility, depending on the quantity of commodity in our possession," which, in developed exchange, gives us the law that Demand, *ceteris paribus*, decreases as Supply increases, and *vice versa*.

A Caveat.—The above analysis corresponds with, and would be recognised by, current ways of thinking and speaking; and, since Jevons, it seems to be accepted by economists. But it may be granted that Utility might be, and has been, defined differently—as the potentiality of satisfying human want; in which case we might speak of Intrinsic Utility. Here Utility would not rise and fall, but be measured by the properties useful to man which things contain; it would correspond, then, with certain fixed physical elements. But such nomenclature leads us into the same difficulties as "intrinsic value" does; and we should in any case require another word to designate

Utility in Jevons' sense. It might be advisable, however, where clearness is required, to speak of Economic Utility.

Total Utility.—On these lines there is suggested one way of measuring Utility. Taking ten successive increments of a similar good, the whole stock may be figured as a sum in addition of Diminishing Utilities, say, 10, 9, 8, 7, 6, 5, 4, 3, 2, 1—a total of 55 units of Utility.

Total Value.—Though it may be suspected that Value is somehow connected with Utility, it is clear that the Total Value of such a stock is not the same as its Total Utility, but something much less. Water, *e.g.*, in spite of the fact that successive increments generally give utilities (though diminishing utilities), is valued at nothing. Supposing the units in the above sum were gallons of water, and an 11th gallon were to be added—representing superfluity as regards wants—the Total Utility would still be 55, as the final utility of 0 does not alter the sum in addition. And yet the Total Value, as men call value or as measured by any canon of purchase or exchange, would be 0. This suggests the solution.

Final Utility and Value.—The value of a stock of goods is measured by the Least or Final Utility—the utility of the last increment. The value of the single good is the Final Utility, and the Total Value is the sum of the Final Utilities. In the above illustrations, the value of each of the ten goods is 1, and the Total Value is 10 ; the value of each of the eleven goods, on the other hand, is 0, and the Total Value likewise is 0. The test always is : If you lose one item, how much value do you lose? You lose only the least utility, and, seeing that value cannot be greater than utility, and that all the items are equal, the utility you lose expresses the value.

Two Objections.—(1) It may be objected that there is an assumption here, namely, that Value is not differential like

Utility. We need to be reminded that we are dealing with human valuations, and that, in such valuation, Value is not differential. When men speak of things having " different values but one price," what they mean is " different utilities but one value"; things of the one objective value or price have different subjective utilities. We certainly find differential values in this sense, that sometimes one man is charged more than another if his pocket can be forced by necessity or his ability to pay is known. But this is exceptional, and, in any case, it does not apply to one and the same man buying successive items of the same goods. (2) It may be objected, in the case of the eleven gallons of water, that it would not generally be acknowledged that the total value was nothing although the loss of one gallon involved no loss of utility, the proof being that, if the total stock is lost, a considerable value is lost. But this is to value the eleven gallons together, considering them as a *single* good, whereas we are considering them as eleven separate goods with diminishing utilities attached to each. The absence of value in the eleven gallons, in short, depends on them being considered not as one stock of water, but as eleven separate gallons.

The Paradox of Value.—From this measurement of value by Final Utility, comes the paradox that the addition of items of goods is an addition of value only up to a certain point: if carried beyond, the Total Value falls; and, if superfluity is reached, it disappears. Taking the former figures; as the items successively increase from 1 to 11, the Total Value describes this course—10, 18, 24, 28, 30, 30, 28, 24, 18, 10, 0; that is to say, an up-grade till the stock consists of five goods, equality between a stock of five and a stock of six, then a down-grade to zero. Thus one may have less Total Value with many goods than with few. The explanation is, as before, that, as goods increase, wants diminish ; the satisfaction dependent on the last added increment is always less than that dependent on the earlier increments—that is, the Final Utility falls ; till, in superfluity, no satisfaction is dependent on one item, and the Value of the single item has disappeared because its Utility has disappeared.

Illustration.—Take the wheat crop in France in 1817, 1818, 1819. The harvest was successively 48, 53, and 64 millions of hectolitres (and presumably the Total Utility increased), while the Total Value was successively 2,046,000,000, 1,442,000,000, and 1,117,000,000 francs. This should remind us that the effort of the industrial world, as distinguished from that of the individual, is always towards the increase of Utility, not necessarily of Value. The total disappearance of Value, however, is almost never seen, because, at the worst, articles however useless subjectively, have always the use of exchange.

The Course of Total Value.—As a rule, Total Value increases with Total Utility, though not in the same proportion : the reason being that there are very few things of which the community, as distinguished from the individual, ever has more than enough to satisfy its most urgent wants. As goods increase, the dependence of the richer classes on them indeed diminishes, but they then come within reach of poorer people, whose want has hitherto been entirely unsatisfied. Thus an abundant crop, although the Final Utility may be low, is *generally* of much greater Total Value than a short one.

Marginal Utility.—As there are many closely related wants, and as the satiation of one would prevent the emergence of others, it is seldom that we completely satisfy any single want. As one want is being satisfied, it diminishes in urgency till there comes a point when another want, not originally so urgent, becomes more urgent ; and having satisfied one want partially, we pass on to the satisfaction of another, and so on successively from want to want, describing a marginal line in the satisfaction of each. This is generally—though perhaps doubtfully—described by saying that, on this line, the marginal utilities are equal. For this reason we replace the expression Final or Least Utility—which is apt to suggest satiation or zero—by the expression, Marginal Utility—the margin at which we stop in the circumstances.

Exchange.—Hitherto Value has been presented as a relation between Satisfactions and Goods. It remains to say that this subjective valuation beomes objective and explicit in exchange; we have, in fact, a definite expression of this valuation in the thing surrendered in exchange. In other words, we need not measure Value by the subjective satisfaction we should lose in losing the marginal item—we actually do lose the utility we part with in purchasing, and this—generally money—names the value. If exchange were by barter, it would be clear that the exchanger surrendered a utility as well as gained one. Take a shepherd and goatherd bartering successive items of their flocks; the gain and loss of sheep-utility and goat-utility are quite evident—as is also the diminishing marginal utility of the items successively acquired and the increasing marginal utility of the items successively parted with. When money forms the one side of the exchange, it is not essentially different; the motive always is that the thing purchased is considered of greater utility than the money parted with : that is to say, of greater utility than all the things that might, in the circumstances, have been purchased with the money. But, in this case, the money parted with expresses universally the value of the goods bought, and gets the name of Price. Thus Price, in this point of view, is the money expression of Marginal Utility.

Marginal Utility of Money.—Money, like all other

goods, diminishes in utility with increase in the amount of it possessed. But the diminution is much less marked, and never comes near zero, because money is not one commodity, satisfying one want, but is potentially, everything that money can buy, *i.e.*, a complex of things satisfying almost the whole complex of wants. Till we have no need for anything which money can buy, the marginal utility of money will not sink to zero.

Demand Price.—What we have in actual life is not, of course, individual bargains between two persons, where the exchange would be determined by the marginal utility on each side, and Demand Price and Supply Price would be convertible terms. Still what we have, on the one side, is multitudes of people—each with different valuations based on different subjective marginal utilities depending on different circumstances of want and provision—offering Demand Prices. That they are confronted, in the market, with another distinct set of prices brings us to the other side of the total theory of value.

Summing Up.—We have, then, passed from Happiness to Satisfaction of Wants and Desires, and from Satisfaction to the Goods which condition it. From this emerges Utility, and the analysis of Utility yields up Total Utility and Marginal Utility. With Marginal Utility we identify Value. Then we found Value naming itself in something given up; that something, in developed civilisations, is Money, and Price becomes the universal expression of Value. When we conceive of Price as the sum of money seeking after goods, it is Demand or Demand Price.

Demand and Supply.—The above is the Theory of Value from one side, that of Demand, *i.e.*, of Utility expressed and measured in money figures, and offering itself as demand for other utilities. It accounts for our willingness to pay certain prices. But although the tap root of value is Utility—for there can be no value in the absence of Utility—there is another side. The sum we are willing to offer—our Demand Price—is confronted with, and at all times affected by, another sum, which seems independent—Supply Price, and this latter sum seems determined by Cost of Production. These two sides and their mutual relations are necessary for any complete Theory of Value. Hence Marshall's words: "There has been a long controversy as to whether Cost of Production or Utility governs Value. It might as reasonably be disputed whether it is the upper or the lower blade of a pair of scissors that cuts a piece of paper."

INDEX

Adam Smith, 1, 8, 18, 20.
Aristotle, 3, 47.
Austrian School, 5, 27, 30, 55, 85.

Böhm-Bawerk, 7, 32, 37, 40, 45, 47, 55, 60, 61.

Complementary goods, 42.
Consumption goods, 68.
Cost of production, 67; conduction of value from marginal products to, 74; from, to products, 78.

Demand Side of the Theory of Value, Appendix II., 91.
Desirable and desired, 10, 11.

Exchange, 56; motives of, 56; isolated, 57; no one-sided competition, 58; ordinary, 58.

Goods, 11, 16; economic, 17; classification of, 21; complementary, 42; stand midway between production and consumption, 68.

Illustrations: sailor and his dog, 30; Crusoe and his sacks, 32; housewife and her butter, 39; silk substitute, 76.

Jevons, 6, 8, 11, 32, 85.

Life, 4, 10.

Marginal buyer, 64; marginal pair, 60, 64.
Marginal products, conduction of value to productive goods, 74.
Marginal utility, 29; level of, 40.
Menger, 11, 15, 17, 42, 45, 68.
Mill, 2.

Neumann, 7.

Political Economy, based on economic conduct, 9.
Price, 55; assumptions of the law, 56; based on subjective valuations, 61; determined by the marginal buyer, 64.

Ricardo, 12, 18.
Roscher, 68.
Ruskin, 4.

Satisfaction, the diminishing scale (*Sättigungscala*), 27; Appendix I., 87.
Scarcity, 10, 11, 16, 40.
Schäffle's objection, 36.
Subjective exchange value, 47; money the typical example, 50.

Supply and Demand, relation of the Austrian law to the law of, 65, 84.
Sydney Smith, 2, 3.

Useful and valuable, the distinction emerging, 11.
Utility, 8, 12; the supreme principle, 13, 14, 24; marginal, 29; the foreign, 39.

Value, looseness of the term, 1; in use and in exchange, 2; not an inherent property, 3; always a relation, 5; subjective and objective, 5; depends entirely on utility, 8; analysis of common usage, 9; the common element, 10; difference from utility, 11, 12; attaches to a felt condition, 14; the centre within us, 16; a relation of dependence, 17; scale of, 18; Adam Smith's scale, 20; where nearly true, 24; the true scale, 26; determined by marginal utility, 32; paradox of, 34; necessity of defining what one is valuing, 35; capitalised, 37; the lowest use, 37; the foreign utility, 39; of complementary goods, 42; subjective exchange, 47; transition to objective, 52; and price, 55; price based on subjective valuations, 61; supply and demand, 65; cost of production, 67; from the past or the future of goods, 67; the conduction of, 70; shown by silver, 72; conducted from marginal products to cost, 74; and from cost to product, 78, 84; the fundamental law, 84

Walker, 4.
Wants, a demand for satisfaction, 15; classification of, 19; scale of, 20.
Wieser, 13, 28, 32, 45, 46, 47, 51, 62, 87.

LargePrintLiberty.com

Dedicated to offering books on libertarian thought and economics in Large Print paperback.

Titles include:

For a New Liberty, by Murray N. Rothbard (Philosophy)
"A classic that for over two decades has been hailed as the best general work on libertarianism available. Rothbard begins with a quick overview of its historical roots, and then goes on to define libertarianism as resting 'upon one single axiom: that no man or group of men shall aggress upon the person or property of anyone else.' He writes a withering critique of the chief violator of liberty: the State. Rothbard then provides penetrating libertarian solutions for many of today's most pressing problems, including poverty, war, threats to civil liberties, the education crisis, and more."

Principles of Economics, by Carl Menger (Economics)
"In the beginning, there was Menger. It was this book that reformulated, and really rescued, economic science. It kicked off the Marginalist Revolution, which corrected theoretical errors of the old classical school. These errors concerned value theory, and they had sown enough confusion to make the dangerous ideology of Marxism seem more plausible than it really was. Menger set out to elucidate the precise nature of economic value, and root economics firmly in the real-world actions of individual human beings."

Great Wars and Great Leaders, by Ralph Raico (History)
"In the backdrop of this blistering and deeply insightful and scholarly history is the whitewashing of 'great leaders' like Woodrow Wilson, Winston Churchill, FDR, Truman, Stalin, Trotsky, and other collectivists. They are highly regarded because they were on the 'right side' of the rise of the state. But do they deserve adulation? Raico says no: these great leaders were main agents in the decline of civilization in the 20th century, all of them anti-liberals who used their power to celebrate and enhance state power."

www.ingramcontent.com/pod-product-compliance
Lightning Source LLC
Chambersburg PA
CBHW080302180526

45167CB00006B/2637